SOME ROOTS OF MODERN ARCHITECTURE

by Heinz Rasch

translated and edited by George and Joan Jelinek

LONDON / ALEC TIRANTI / 1967

TRANSLATORS' NOTE

Dr. Rasch has written these articles and lectures over a period of forty years but it will be found that they are true in architectural thought and feeling to his main period of the 1920s and early 1930s.

His objective viewpoint, coupled with his personal knowledge and involvement in the modern architectural movement in Germany, give us a new and deeper insight into the original thought processes and their evolution during this vital period.

The attitudes of mind towards architecture which come across so well in the author's German text will, therefore, be of great interest to architects today.

PRINTED BY PORTLAND PRESS LTD., LONDON WI
BOUND BY C. & H. T. EVANS LTD., CROYDON

MADE AND PRINTED IN THE UNITED KINGDOM
GB SBN 85458-040

CONTENTS

INTRODUCTION

Architectural schools of the past taught the new generation of architects to imitate the historic examples of the past and especially, in the last century, the Gothic and Renaissance styles. To these were added, at the beginning of our own century, Egyptian, Islamic, Indian and Far Eastern examples, so that in 1924, in the famous Guildhall in Stockholm, an almost complete 'museum' was produced composed of all the different styles from all the various periods.

These different historic styles were obstacles to the development of new building materials such as steel and concrete and to their related technology, since they were based on the building techniques of stone, brick, and timber. But in the end, with the broadening of this historic view, it was realised that architecture encompassed a far wider field, so that more and more simple and fundamental examples were sought—buildings of the Middle Ages, farmhouses, especially in the Mediterranean. Mies van der Rohe's lecture to the B.D.A. in 1925 began with a picture of an Eskimo igloo. And from here we did not have far to go to reach all the appliances, and indeed the entire extent, of nature and technology. Imitation of outstanding achievements of the architectural past had shown itself to be a shallow and meaningless process.

Now we looked for the 'essence', as we called it, and we started to adopt a new point of view. Until 1923 it was believed that architecture had to be thought of in terms of plastic art. The circle and the square, the sphere and the cube, were basic design principles (Sullivan, Berlage, Peter Behrens). Perspectives disappeared and models were substituted. After 1923, however, we realised that the appearance of a building was less important than the usefulness of its internal spaces. From this point in time function became more important than structure (Frank Lloyd Wright, Van de Velde).

Then in 1922 the first new architectural precept was proposed: *Space is direction* (taught and promoted by architects such as Mendelsohn, Döcker, Mies van der Rohe, Le Corbusier). Two years later a second precept was added: *Space is resistance*. Structures in steel and reinforced concrete had become the basis of modern architecture (Corbusier, Mies van der Rohe, Mart Stam, were the most striking pioneers). In 1927 at the time of the Weissenhofsiedlung in Stuttgart and the first Zeilensiedlung of the Dammerstock competition in Karlsruhe, the third precept was added: *Space is distance*, whereby the horizontal planes (ceilings and floors) are characterised in terms

1

of a finite primary system, and the walls in terms of a changeable, flexible secondary system, and the screen is adopted as the fundamental basic (Rietfeld, Mies van der Rohe, Gropius, Häseler). This was followed in 1929 by a further precept: *Space is perception*, whereby the spatial boundaries are brought into harmony with the sense organs and their extensions (Mies van der Rohe, Schlemmer, Baumeister). Much later, after the Second World War, a fifth precept was pioneered: *Space is path*, meaning that space is basically a 'motion space' concerned with the intention of bringing order into the motion of objects (Scharoun, Krause, Schwagenscheid).

In this book all the phases of this theoretical structure are illustrated by works and publications of the time. The lectures which follow show the significance of our five precepts. *The Absolute and Modulation* deals on the one hand with space and with what has become standard, and on the other hand with natural phenomena and what is individual—in other words, a new way of looking at the world. *The Mastery of Technology* points out structural consequences and at the same time takes a look into the future.

However, study of the history of building and building styles has not therefore lost its value. Architectural memorials, like all the products of human ingenuity, powers of discovery and creation, form part of the fundamental knowledge and training of our feeling for order and form.

1. THE CIRCLE AND THE SQUARE

A lecture given at Kassel, 27th January 1966

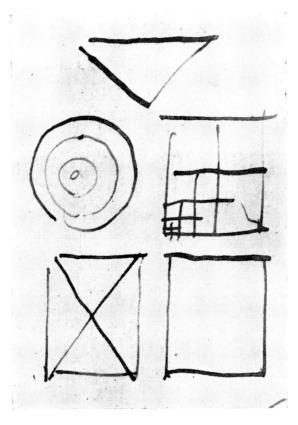

1   *Drawing by Oskar Schlemmer*

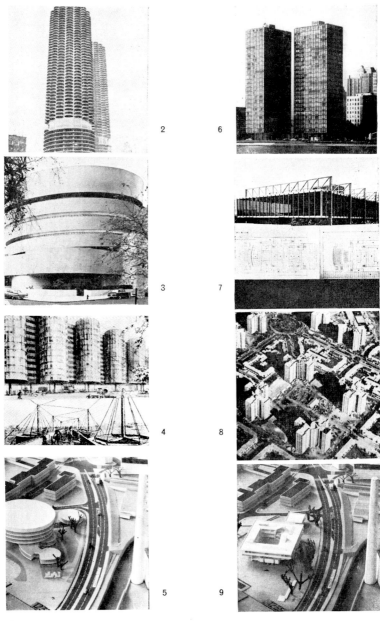

2

6

3

7

4

8

5

9

4

INTRODUCTION

The circle and the square are basic shapes which, when used as elements in the design of buildings and tools, can lead to totally different results.

Originally the use of these shapes was determined by the material and the type of construction; then, due to the influence of the baroque, they were used very freely. But at the beginning of this century, when people began to question the meaning and purpose of the immense number of different shapes of roofs, buildings, spaces and appliances, the circle and the square became recognised points of departure, and at the same time there was an almost universal recognition of their significance.

The *Jugendstil* saw in the circle the symbol of the phenomena of nature; the *Werkbund* saw the square as the basis of their 'universal order of things'. Later on it seemed unavoidable that the two shapes should be segregated and that a choice should be made between them. The circle, with its polygonal derivatives, stood as the symbol for life reform and a revival of romanticism as well as expressionism; the square, and in a wider sense the rectangle, symbolised socialism as well as the classic bias of cubism.

Towards the end of the period of inflation the circle and the polygon lost support because they stood for individualism and, not least, because of their **2–9**

10

11

---

2 GOLDBERG. Tower blocks of flats, Chicago 1962

3 F. Ll. WRIGHT. Guggenheim Museum, New York 1952

4 H. RASCH. Project of point blocks of flats with suspension structures, 1955

5 H. RASCH. Sketch design for a civic centre, 1962

6 MIES VAN DER ROHE. Blocks of flats, Chicago 1960

7 MIES VAN DER ROHE. Sketch design for a theatre, Manheim 1952

8 Housing scheme, New York 1951

9 WILL BALTZER. Sketch design for a civic centre, 1963

10 FRANZ KRAUSE. Private House, 1948

11 LE CORBUSIER. Church at Ronchamps, 1953

5

limited application. Curves disappeared from sketch designs and the multiform pitched roof lost in the highly emotional battle against the flat roof. But lately these shapes and forms have reappeared, in the form of polygonal and circular concert halls and churches, circular point blocks, sharp-angled bungalows—quite apart from all the curves found in everything to do with transport and communications. The reason for this is exactly the same as before: man, yoked to the order-system of the rectangle, needs to escape—nowadays even with the help of his car.

When we wonder whether we are dealing here with a transitional phenomenon or with a true phase of development, we need to review yet again a few ideas from the 1920s, if only to find out how they differ from those of today. This can be done by considering four quotations from four essays: *Der Architekturfilm* (The Film about Architecture; München-Augsburger Abendzeitung 1924), which deals with the generation of space in terms of the expansion of a nucleus of matter; *Material, Construction, Form* ('Baugilde', 1925), dealing with the transience of individual forms; *Crisis in Architecture* (radio lecture, 1926; printed in Steinholzeisen), dealing with the additive and divisive system of rectangle; together with the flexible arrangement of walls and the umbrella and suspension houses taken from the editions of *Wie Bauen* dated 1927 and 1928. The following observations, derived from the contents of these essays, have been divided into two sections: Mass, and Function.

10–13

12

13

12 *WOLFGANG RATHKE. Lattice roof construction for an exhibition pavilion, 1965*

13 *HANS SCHAROUN. Philharmonie Berlin 1963*

MASS

14 *Drawing by Oskar Schlemmer*

1. The Circle The circle belongs to our earliest impressions: the moon, sun, eyes, mouth, apple, cup, boss, bowl, pillar, pipe. Cézanne is reported as saying that one can reduce all that's seen to the three circular forms, the sphere, the cone, and the cylinder, and from these can form a picture of his surroundings. In fact, it is possible to find the circular form in almost all natural objects, so much so that some people would like to look upon the circle as the symbol of self enclosed mass—everyone is familiar with the term 'circular' used of a matter or argument, meaning a circle which closes itself—

15–16

7

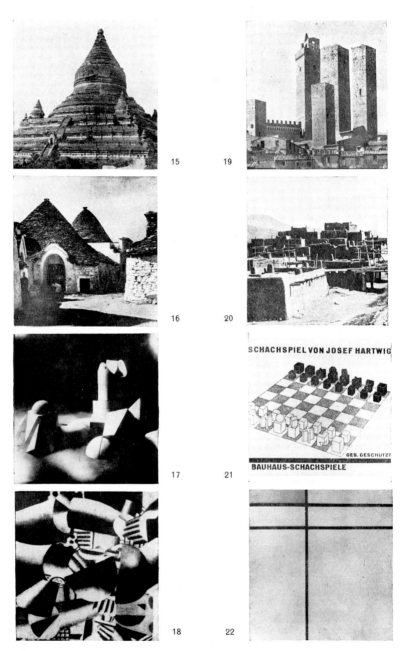

15

19

16

20

17

21

SCHACHSPIEL VON JOSEF HARTWIG

GES. GESCHUTZT

BAUHAUS-SCHACHSPIELE

18

22

since the circle is finitely limited in terms of its concept. However large one may consider the circle to be, two radii, **R1** and **R2**, are still connected with a portion of the circumference which because of this is designated as finite. And since each curved line closes into a circle when infinitely extended, even this line, in contradistinction to the straight line, is invariably finite.

Even symmetry, which is one of the most striking peculiarities of circular bodies, excludes the concept of unlimited expansion. With a symmetrical division, each portion is represented twice and both refer back to the centre

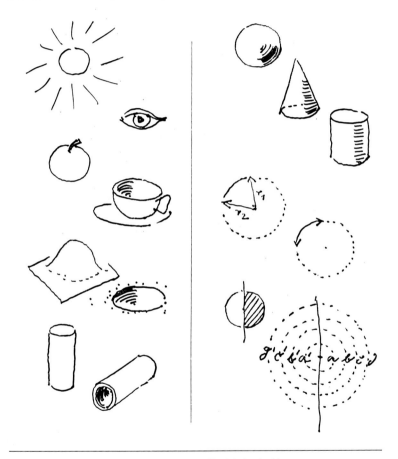

15 Dagaba in Pagan
16 Trullos in Apulia
17 HERMANN FINSTERLIN. Set of children's building blocks

18 Painting by Lèger
19 Towers of San Gimignano
20 Pueblos at Taos, USA
21 Bauhaus chess set
22 Painting by Mondrian

about which they exist in equilibrium. If these symmetrical portions were not limited in their expansion it would mean that the centre, positioned within the circle, could be displaced at random without altering the equilibrium. Even the mirror image repetition of a series of different forms, **A, B, C, D,** signifies nevertheless only finite circles with radii **A** (in the mirror image **A'**), or **B** (in the mirror image **B'**).

The finite quality of the circle permits its division. Division of the circle is made by means of its radii and results in triangles similar to slices cut from a cake. Assuming that these sectors are regular, their number determines the polygon so made. The circle is a polygon consisting of an infinite number of

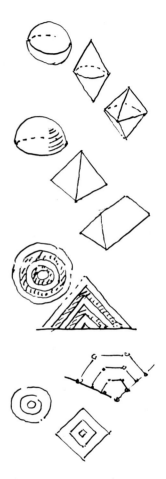

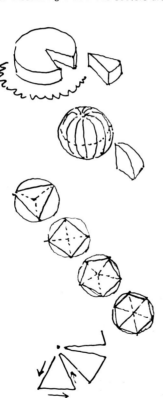

such triangles. The same goes for the sphere. The division of an orange results in wedge shaped slices. Then, if one further cuts the orange across in half, one obtains halved segments which, if the curvature is disregarded, become tetrahedra. In this way the triangle is demonstrated to be the element of the circle. Triangles or sectors consisting of two radii and an arc are arranged side by side with their points coinciding in a common centre. The circle, and all polygons, whether they be three-, four-, five- or six-sided,

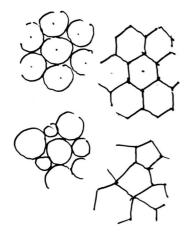

or more, are always made up of triangles. Moreover, in circumscribing the individual triangles one always has to go back to the centre: that is, starting from the centre, one goes along radius number one, then continues along the arc, and then returns back along radius number two to the centre. The triangular step of the waltz always leads back to its point of origin: it is therefore a revolving dance step in contrast to the march.

In this manner, therefore, all polygonal forms must be classified as derivatives of the circle. The pyramid and the hipped roof are relatives of the dome—for example, Taut's polehedric cupola for the Glashaus in Cologne, the dome of the Schauspielhaus by Poelzigs, the roof of the Wylerberghaus by Bartning, and the Geotheaneum at Dornach. If the size of these forms is increased or decreased, they demon-

strate the same central relationship, for this change in size occurs in layers: on the one hand like the increase by rolling of a large snowball, or the building of a pyramid, or the growth of a crystal (the mathematician may even think of polygonal numbers); and on the other hand like the shaving off of timber chips by the joiner, or the erosion of stone and metal due to weathering. All enlargements lead to a central aggregation. In decorating a cake, each added piece is forced into a relationship with the middle in order to produce an evenly-spaced arrangement. This applies to all polygons, even to the square in so far as it is fixed as a central form by its diagonals, that is, its radii. (Behrens, Oldenberg, 1904.) **27**

2. The Square. We see our surroundings **19–22** as a mosaic of forms in juxtaposition, and so naturally it is in this manner that we think of Cézanne's sphere, cone, and cylinder, as well as the two-dimensional forms which result from their relevant sections, the circle, the triangle, and the rectangle.

Circles cannot be fitted next to each other without leaving gaps. When they are nevertheless forced closer together, circles of the same size are transformed into hexagons, and circles of varying size result in the formation of varied polygons (see basalt). The perfect fitting together of equal polygons succeeds only in the case of the triangle, the square, and the hexagon. The triangle is also found to be the basis of the square and the hexagon. In the case of the hexagon the triangles are arranged about a centre, and for this reason it is the only form similar to the circle which can be fitted together without leaving any gaps. It is also similar to the circle in that, in multiple combination, it is impossible to build a larger composite form of the same shape as

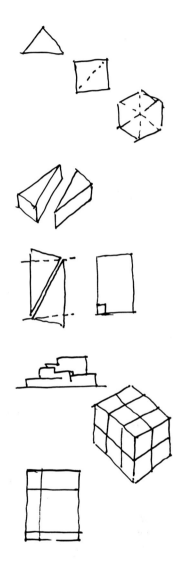

that of the smaller subordinate hexagon.

The square is formed by triangles in the same way as a pastrycook arranges two triangular pieces of cake next to each other in a package. In this case the centre is ignored by the radii of the two sectors, so that two triangles are always fitted together in opposite directions. They can be traced in outline in one uninterrupted line, and continued indefinitely in the form of a folded strip. The parallelogram thus created can be transformed without any difficulty into a rectangle (the case of the octahedron is similar). Each rectangle can be assembled out of squares and can be split up into squares.

The square, when multiplied, results in the formation of still more squares; and, assuming that the first square is infinitely small, this makes possible any desired combination or permutation, stretching into infinity, as large or as small in any part as one might wish, and which can be still further added to or multiplied. They can be increased in number, like salt crystals, pueblos, and the sculptures of Malevich, and can be split up, like the various compartments of a large travelling case, or a printer's type case, or a property split up into plots, or the pictures of Mondrian.

In this instance, instead of enclosed or total forms, we have only rectangular, interrelated straight lines and planes (furrows in a field, various textures of wickerwork or mesh) from which it would be impossible to discover what object we are dealing with, if the material itself, of which they are composed, did not disclose this fact. Not

23

27

24

28

25

29

26

30

13

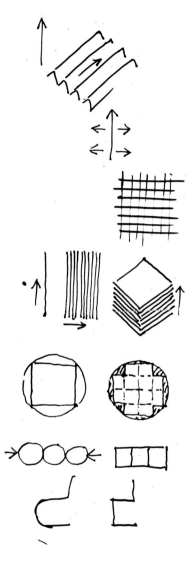

The square is therefore looked upon as a form with universal application (as compared with the circle, which one could describe as an isolated form). It is therefore a basic element of the universal law of order; and for this reason it has been the aim of mankind since ancient times to square the circle. Purely geometrically, this cannot be achieved without a remainder. Moreover when a circle is completely filled with the most minute squares, tiny corners remain, as for instance in the apportionment of the curved hull of a ship. With quantitative gain, however, spherical lumps of dough laid next to each other undergo peripheral gain when the dough rises, and become cubical dumplings; and with quantitative reduction fragments of stone (even cube shaped ones) become spherical pebbles in the brook. Whilst maintaining

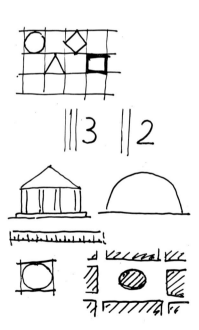

the form but the material is the criterion for differentiation, and under the term 'material' we would include especially its colour.

14

31 BRUNO TAUT. Glashaus, Cologne 1914

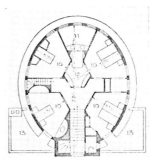

32 PETER BEHRENS. Villa, 1904

their quantity, spherical dried figs or plums become cube shaped through pressure applied in packaging; just as, vice versa, the dough which was formed into cubes becomes circular loaves, and, in the technical world, many circular items change their shapes into rectangular ones. The circular washing machine becomes rectangular. The old sugar loaf has become the sugar cube. The form of traffic vehicles such as buses and ships, originally bellied-out, has now been transformed into a cubic one; and, in contrast to the curvilinear form of Mies van der Rohe's tubular steel chair, the cubic chair by Mart Stam achieved success.

Only rectangular forms permit combination into larger units. In order to fit the circle into a square system one must surround it with a square, like packing a football into a square box. Then it is possible to fit the boxes together without leaving any gaps, and thus, from the isolated forms, produce unified elements. Seen in this way, one cannot even argue with Cézanne when he fits his circular forms, spheres, cones and cylinders, together, since they would be situated so to say inside the squares or cubes of the boxes into which Cézanne divides his picture plane. He does this in the knowledge that man, standing perpendicular to the horizontal plane, is consequently subconsciously aware of the theme of rectangular space which runs through all the forms of nature: so much so that rectangular forms, walls, signs, and pictures, function naturally and interrelatedly, whereas those forms which deviate, such as triangles, rhomboids, and circles, separate themselves and attract attention—a fact commonly made use of in traffic

33 Exhibition hall, Berlin 1931

signals. Like these signs, the circular shapes of arabic numerals jump out at one, in comparison with the abstract structures of roman numerals, as do cupolas compared with colonnades.

The rectangular lines and planes of the square run to infinity without limitation. Each portion is interchangeable. The square is merely the measure —'to measure' means simply to square up. There is no centre. Because of this the circle, with its principle of finiteness, is placed within the square, with its principle of infinity, not vice versa (see Behrens' circular *Haus der Frau* situated in the square plot in the grounds of the Berlin Building Exhibition, 1931, and the oval house on a rectangular site which was a student scheme in 1922).

FUNCTION

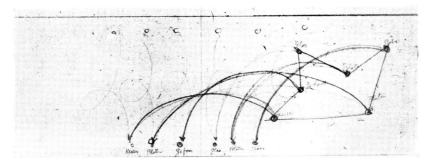

34 OSKAR SCHLEMMER.   *Choreographic sketches for Bauhaus ballet*

1. Expansion. The development of line from dot, plane from line, and mass from plane occurs through multiplication, that is, a moving of the objects in a forward direction, or, quite commonly, through action. Because of action, for instance, circular ripples are created when one throws a stone into water; the size of the circles of the ripples indicates the sphere of action. We speak of a sphere of action in connection with a volcanic eruption, or with a source of light, noise, or smell. For us, the concept of the sphere of action is inborn, not least because we stand at the centre of our environment, which lies about us rather like the ripples in the water; the arm hanging in the ball joint on our shoulder describes a circle, and thereby the extent of our environment which it can reach. The earth hangs from the invisible arm of the sun, the moon from that of the earth, and the sphere of action is circumscribed by the orbit of the earth, or again by that of the moon. The sphere of action determines the circumference of the circle. Man, who in all his thoughts and actions tends to refer to himself as being the nearest example of a sym-

35

36

37

38

metrical body, 'carves out his cell, in that he creates all around him barriers which he then pushes outwards. Space is created in terms of the expansion of a nucleus of matter.'

This concept presupposes space filled with substance in which the boundaries consist of the internal expansion forces and the external resistance forces. If the substance is uniform the boundaries form a sphere: as with hailstones, berries, planets, also air balloons, bathyscapes, and cupolas. If the substance is made up of differing elements, this results in the creation of irregular forms such as caves, clouds, or potatoes, which accordingly have to be regarded as distortions of the circle. The process of expansion is a matter either of the positive or of the negative, that is, either the pudding or the pudding basin. The pudding we regard as a 'body' and talk of its circumference; the pudding basin is designated as 'space', and we speak of its content. We call a cave a space and a potato a body. In the case of a cupola we combine both concepts, depending on whether we regard it as a space (Hagia Sophia) or as a body (as for instance in the case of the massive cupolas of the Indian Stupas). The cave form we call 'concave' and the bulbous form 'convex'. Two convex forms belong to two different bodies and when they touch each other it is in a single spot—like two steel balls, which for this reason can never be stacked one on top of another. Because of this, the convex form is generally used in cases where it is a matter of repulsing another body, as, for example, curvilinear bridge piles and the bows of a ship are designed to deal with water currents or icefloes,

3

3

---

35 *MIES VAN DER ROHE. Traffic control tower, 1925*
36 *Recess in the Jugendhat house*
37 *H. & B. RASCH. Shell-concrete project for a house, 1928*
38 *H. & B. RASCH. Chair made of bent plywood, 1928*

chimney pots and lighthouses with the wind, bastions with enemy attacks. Two concave forms, however, invariably combine into a single body.

We therefore connect the concave form with the concept 'interior' and the convex form with the concept 'exterior'.

But whether they are spatial forms or body forms, both alike owe their existence to the process of expansion. Layer upon layer grow the sand heap and the stalactite, layer upon layer grows the cave or the inner surface of a vessel made by the potter at his wheel or the joiner at his lathe. Here the hand is the corporeal nucleus which creates the space, like an excavator working in a sandpit or opencast mine. If the vessel is meant to be spherical in shape, the hand applies an even pressure in all directions, always closely moulded to the surface as the pudding is to the pudding basin. When hollowing out a cylindrical container, the hand moves downwards, adding one ring to the next as it moves, and building in sequence. The same applies when the hollow space is to be cone-shaped. The child's

19

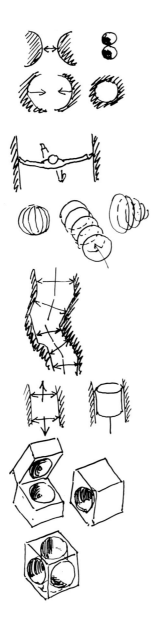

hand excavates a cylindrical tunnel in his sand castle or a conical hollow in the sand. The motion downwards creates a 'motion space'. The hand can be withdrawn quite smoothly from the tunnel or the cone.

So we are dealing here with two expansion components: sideways, and straight ahead. If we put a person into this space and make him the source point of expansion, we can see that his sideways expansion is determined by his arms, but that his legs permit him to leave the central focal point, and that, whilst the reach of the arms is strictly limited, the action of the legs, even if only in principle, is unlimited. 'When the centre is moved, a longish shape is formed which can be wider or thinner depending on the rate of motion. A mole's tunnel in the earth, or a branch suspended in the air—in this way we can also imagine the creation of the streets and squares of an ancient town.' A child's sand castles are equivalent to walled structures, caves, and Eskimo igloos. A case made for a crystal ball consists of two hemispherical halves; when the two halves are put together, the hollow space is enclosed on all sides. Or a piece of timber can be drilled from one side to the other (tunnel), then again at right-angles (crossvault), and finally drilled again from top to bottom, leaving us with a mushroom-shaped hollow space, which in this case is simply duplicated and trebled and left open to the exterior. Yet in each instance we are dealing with hollow spaces whose surfaces or walls are related to an internal centre point or axis.

Technology substantiates the creation of space by expansion. 'The flat wall has to be buttressed, the curved one contains its own stability within its form; the flat roof has to be supported, the vaulted roof is self-supporting and sufficient by itself. This is because a curved body extends in three dimen-

20

sions and therefore becomes a three-dimensional body.'

In the instances of the sphere and the cylinder these 'rings of expansion' are equal, but in the cone they diminish or increase with every single forward motion, and this makes the alterations

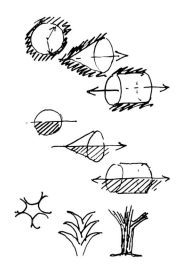

in the internal force relationships visible. If one cuts each of these three bodies through the middle with a flat plane, then one discovers in the upper half familiar space forms such as cupolas and barrels, and in the lower half structural shells like ships' hulls, or, in the case of a single-sided framework (like a sugar scoop), cantilevered floors fixed to the pillars like the branches to a tree trunk, or even the shape of a chanterelle mushroom or an agave (funnels or fan-vaults of English Gothic architecture). See the plywood chairs of 1924 and the shell house with umbrella structure from the book *Wie Bauen?*

*   *   *

2. *Relationship.* The example of the sphere, cylinder, and cone being hollowed out by the hand can be expanded to a larger scale: a mass of people milling about a centre of attraction, being held back by a chain of policemen which presses backwards in order to stem the tide, in a circular shape about a static centre or else in two rows, one on each side of a street, when a procession is held—this path widening out in a conical shape from the entrance portico and becoming wider as the amount of spectator resistance lessens. The forward-pressing mass of people indicates the forces which act upon a space, the backs of the policemen form the space enclosure, which can therefore be called 'private space'. This enclosure or shell is like an open vessel. Opposite the open end is the 'prospect space'. (Press Conference

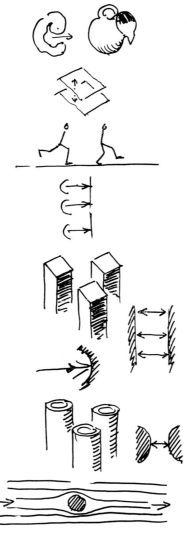

wide view through the window soothes.')

The terms 'private space' and 'prospect space', in that each always applies to only one half of a space (in other words the opposite and facing boundaries of a space), clearly define the relationship between two objects, or, more precisely, between their surfaces which are turned towards each other. This means that these two surfaces either lie parallel to each other or must maintain an equal distance in relation to each other. The surface which the blind man investigates by touch, as for instance when reading Braille, must lie parallel with his organ of touch, i.e. the fingers of his hand must all be the same distance away from the surface. In the same way our feet investigate the ground they walk on, by touch; and when we look in a mirror the object and its reflected image are linked only by the rays of light reflected at right angles to the glass. All horizontal and vertical surfaces occupy a related position, one to the other, as do the rectangular towers of San Gimignano or Manhatten; whilst surfaces which have curved or sharply-angled relationships to each other belong to isolated objects, and for this reason, during the last years of his life, Baumeister proposed using slightly inclined walls for paintings.

Our problem lies in the establishment and the prevention of relationships; the establishment of relationships being brought about by the expansion of our motor and sensory equipment, and the prevention of relationships (as for instance against wind, rain, gravity) by the interpositioning of walls, roofs, floor slabs, etc. Now these relationships are of extremely varied duration. Some last only for a fraction of a second, others endure for the full life span of the earth. And so one must add to the existing three dimensions of space a fourth dimension: time.

Living things and their actions are

36 1926, Mies van der Rohe's semi-circular screen wall in the Tugendhat House, 1930, Ardenauer's interview, 1966: 'The circular form of his work-room induces concentration, but the

which I described earlier, one below the other, or by placing mushroom shapes one on top of the other; and in this case the thickness of the slabs is arbitrary, since one has sufficient room in both the upward and downward direction: the floor slabs are simply flat planes separated vertically from each other. However one could imagine a single storey, very high, with one single roof slab from which other lift slabs are suspended, like grapes from the vine or spiders from their thread—i.e. like hammocks. And since the available height is limited and divided up by the intermediate floor slabs, it becomes necessary to make the floor slabs as thin as possible in order to obtain optimum utilisation: all division approaches zero.

Here we have two forms of expansion, the first in an upward direction in the form of a supporting structure whose height is determined by the limits of the material it is built from—in the same way as a tree—and the second from the top in a downward direction, in terms of a suspended floor slab system—like suspended bookshelves—in which case the suspended planes should be of a minimal material thickness and should be in a sense composed merely of anti-gravity forces. With these storeys, the floor and ceiling slabs are the planes of reference. The floor surface forms the private space and the ceiling becomes the prospect space; just as in our earlier example the chain of policemen represented a commonly shared private space or wall, floor and ceiling have now become, in a vertical relationship, respectively a commonly shared private and prospect space for all objects which are situated on the floor, so that these objects are capable of interchange, that is they can alter their positions. In order that one object may leave the position it occupies, an adjacent position needs to be unoccupied. Then the object alters its

liable to especially swift changes, and our houses and towns are visible evidence of this. 'It is worthwhile to look for buildings which still function today as they did originally and which still accord with their original purpose. Is the architect clear in his own mind how long his design remains valid?' Whilst ground surfaces retain their validity for long periods, walls on the other hand quickly take on the role of obstacles when alterations in the mode of living demand changes. This means that nowadays in architecture emphasis is placed on horizontal planes, and not on the vertical ones as in the past: the floor slabs are the primary system of architecture. These floor slabs are made by the excavation of the hollow spaces

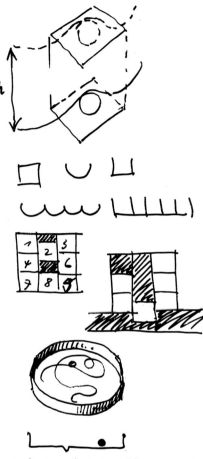

on only one of four different sides, the movement of the counters is jerky, diverging at right angles to its course. The art of interchanging positions lies at the basis of all systems of order—regimens for physical exercise, calculating machines, filing systems and filing cabinets, railway compartments—and Oskar Schlemmer gave artistic expression to this artform of the right-angled interchange of positions in his Bauhaus Ballet. At the same time we still find ourselves within the same system of relationships—one merely walks, as it were, from one room into the next.

This system can also be extended into a three-dimensional casing within which a cube can move not only horizontally but also vertically. Then there is also that other particular point of view, where the space is seen to be determined, not by the trellis or grid of the objects, but merely by the motion itself.

This is clearly demonstrated in the children's puzzle which consists of a flat plane with a series of small ball-bearings rolling around on it. By slight inclinations of the plane, the ball-bearings can be manoeuvred into a series of tiny indentations—a large motion space and a small static space.

And so in the one case we are looking for pathways, and in the other for objects: the pathways in terms of hollow or cave spaces, the objects in terms of the total environment with all its events, the most distant as well as the closest. And just as these things may be infinite, so also are their inter-relationships and our relationships with them. The crazed pattern of these relationships results in an infinite motion space in which the objects float like islands. The earlier concept of space in terms of a hollow or cave is therefore valid only for a single relationship: for a great number, or indeed the totality, of relationships the only concept which remains valid is that of open and endless space filled with an infinite number of

static state into a mobile one and transforms the static space into a motion space. There are only occupied positions and unoccupied positions.

Interrelated alterations of position are the purpose of numerous party games and puzzles, of which I will here mention only two. First we have the sliding puzzles in which counters occupy every little square except one, and this empty place is the motion space provided for sliding the counters. Since the motion space can be situated

24

insular objects. This, then, also results in an architectural concept: 'The city on piloti, which makes all traffic independent of the restricting masses of buildings, is nowadays no longer an imaginary Utopia.'

The concept of space in terms of a relationship between two planes has its starting point with the identity of these planes and the extent of their distance apart as an interaction of force and resistance within the material universe—a supposition which is not contradicted by our own experiences. At some time or another we must all have felt the light switch, the clock or, the pair of slippers, in order to recognise and find them again in the dark. A street or a railway track enables one to trace it back to its starting point. The thread on which the spider lowers itself is the space through which it will once again return. This space is invariably a motion space. Even the retina of the eye selects, from the mosaic of lights and images by which it is interconnected with the external environment, certain specific reference points which we then, judging by experience, mentally push out to the correct distance away. Here two simultaneous processes are involved: an additive pushing out or placing within the material universe, and a divisive measuring of the distance of return.

Still further generalisations could be added, such as the idea of looking upon the 'birth' and 'death' of space as changes in the solidification or attenuation of matter; or perhaps, together with the creation of the universe itself, in terms of an everlasting pulse, or swing of the pendulum—but all that really lies outside our field.

CONCLUSION

Curlicues and geometric figures seen in sketch books of the early 1920s reveal just how much effort we expended in establishing a superposed or, as we then said, a 'fundamental' form for buildings and tools—an effort which, incidentally, no one wanted to admit to afterwards because we demanded only results, and not theories which were in any case looked upon as unscientific so long as no special field of knowledge existed in connection with the technology of space. Nevertheless Mies van der Rohe stressed that such knowledge depends on the intellect, by which he meant a basic theory. He knew very well that in this case one is entirely dependent on one's own personal concepts—and to have concepts is one thing, but to clarify them quite another.

But the effort has been worthwhile. Because of it much has been cleared out of the way. After all the arches, the triangles, and the polygons, the only thing still left in the end was the square. Together with this fact the most important thing was that one had discovered the function behind the forms. In place of the circle, the functional concept 'expansion' was substituted, consisting of static space and motion space, private space and prospect space, from which the space elements of Resistance, Orientation and Route were supposed to spring. The square, however, led to the functional concept of 'relationship', and we learned to recognise relationship, not only in terms of distance, but as experience. From the interplay of the space elements, forms come about of their own accord. In the end a circle, or a square, or both, could be the outcome —forms are not primary!

2. THE ELEMENTS OF SPACE

Lecture given at the Staatlichen Werkkunstschule at Kassel, 15th July 1965

*39   Page from the
sketchbook of Mies
van der Rohe*

*The space which a circle requires,
consists of the square which surrounds it.*

40 CARL GROSBERG. Tenement house in Hanover

Mies van der Rohe (1925), Corbusier and Mart Stam (1926), and earlier as well as later (1924 and 1937) with Franz Krause, Oskar Schlemmer, and Willi Baumeister. Many of these ideas were also contained in the course of architecture taught by Bonatz, Wetzel, and Doecker in 1922-23.

This lecture is therefore also representative of the concepts of that generation. It is presented in the way it developed. The first four sections are taken from the manuscripts of the unpublished 1933 edition of the book *Wie Bauen?* (How to Build?). Section 5 represents the lectures entitled *The Special and the Standard* and *Island Dwellings*, given at Hagen in 1951 and 1954. More detailed information can be found in the books the author published in co-operation with his brother, Brodo Rasch—*Wie Bauen?* of 1927, *Wie Bauen?* of 1928, *Der Stuhl* (The Chair) of 1928, *Zu-Offen* (Closed-Open) and *Gefesselter Blick* (Captive Vision) of 1930.

Towards the middle of the 1920s we began to take our bearings from the things we encountered in everyday life. The First World War had put an end to the social and architectural conception that exteriors of buildings must be made as imposing as possible. We thus found new basic standpoints: the relation between 'inside' and 'outside', supporting and dividing building elements, the apportionment of space, and boundaries; and last but not least, communication between everything describing 'space', that is (1) Orientation, (2) Resistance, (3) Distance, (4) Perception, and (5) Path or route.

Each architect, however, went his own way about it. The author, who took part in this development with works of his own, knows from personal recollection and from drawings in his sketchbook that he was basically of the same opinion as Mendelsohn (1924),

41 Famous façades and roof structures separated from each other

68 42

45

28

42   Page from the author's sketch book, 1924

1. Orientation. Castles placed on high rocks, such as Lichtenstein or Stolzenfils, or lighthouses which are surrounded by water and have been crammed into a narrow space, direct the eye outwards through windows and battlements. Palaces set within parks, like Sanssouci or Amalienburg, form a coherent 'interior'. The castles are characterised by parapets with views over the top, the palaces by recessed rear walls which form the rooms. Both these types are found combined in a circus: the ring corresponds to the parapet space in a   **43, 44**

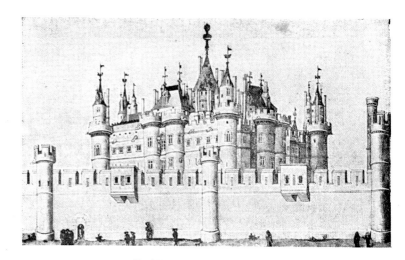

43   Old drawing of the Louvre in Paris

44   Sanssouci, Potsdam

30

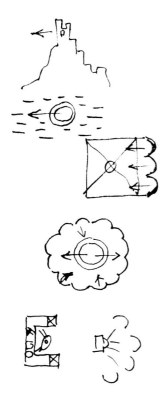

placed at the most exposed edge of the step and the recess space, normally connected with the ground, becoming the triangular recess between tread and riser. Thus the parapet space projects outwards whilst the recess space recedes. This is demonstrated by the interconnecting inclined plane between the upper and lower levels which, in the example of a house, would cor-

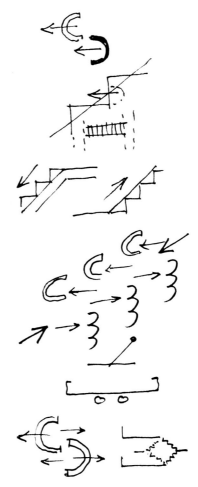

castle (or the altar in a church), the spectators' seats correspond to the recesses of the palace. So we are concerned here with two opposite types of orientation, one directed from the centre outward, and one directed inward. We meet this everywhere—we meet it in our own homes. We find the outward orientation in the kitchen where the housewife is surrounded by narrow working surfaces. The inward one is found in the living room where seats are grouped around the fireplace and the television set. These two rooms are situated next to each other. When arranged vertically one above the other, they become like a step: one can visualise the parapet space as being

31

respond to a straight flight of stairs. The parapet space corresponds to the 'projecting' corners of a stair, and the recess space to the 'receding' ones. One can often see examples of such parapet spaces in old high-lying villages when one is looking upwards at the staggered, projecting gables of the entrance porticos all facing downhill. In low-lying villages on the other hand, when looking up a steeply rising street of houses, one sees recess spaces, formed by the staggered entrances under overhanging eaves, with their sloping sides facing downhill.

91

The expression 'parapet space' needs still further clarification. In a tramcar the driver on the front platform looks outwards, so to say, over the 'parapet'. He therefore stands in a parapet space, whereas the passenger on the rear platform, leaning with his back against the 'parapet' and facing forwards, is standing in a recess space. At the terminus this situation is reversed. Quite how much depends on the direction in which the person is facing becomes even clearer in the example of the diving board. The diving board can be used functionally for diving, i.e. actively, but occasionally it is also used for sunbathing, i.e. passively. These two different orientations for the use of the diving board correspond to two cantilevered plywood chairs made in 1926 which have their spring or 'give' at the front for an active working posture and at the back for a passive reclining posture. In the case of the diving board, the parapet space consists merely of the very edge, just as a balcony would still be a parapet space even without railings. Indeed we find lecturers' podia made either with or without a rail. Instead of 'parapet space', we might define it even better as a 'platform space'.

53

If we look for an even better description of our two opposite space types, we shall find them side by side in the

example of the old-fashioned hansom cab. The driver's seat on top is clearly a parapet or platform space, and the inside of the coach with its upholstered seating in the back is obviously a recess space. The driver's seat is outside, up

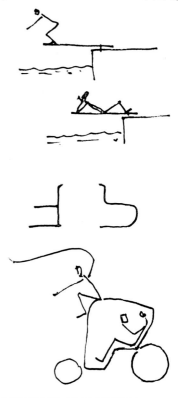

45 ERICH MENDELSOHN. Mossehaus, 1924
46 RICHARD DÖCKER. Bridge across the Neckar, 1925
47 H. SCHAROUN. Competition design for the Münsterplatz, 1925
48 HUGO HÄRING. Plan for a private house, 1924
49 FRANK LI. WRIGHT. Robie House, 1909
50 H. & B. RASCH. Broadcasting house chairs, 1924
51 H. & B. RASCH. House at Bad Oeynhausen, 1926
52 LE CORBUSIER. House at Stuttgart, 1927

45

46

47

48

49

50

51

52

33

on the box. We shall call this position the 'reach' space, as it is from here that he reaches outwards into space. The passenger, however, sits inside the coach container as if he were inside a cave, and we shall therefore define this enclosed space as the 'cave' space. Take another example from a seaside holiday: if one stands on top of a mound of sand when the tide comes in, this mound then becomes a 'reach' space; whereas the moat of a sand-castle is a 'cave' space.

53   H. & B. RASCH. Chair, 1927

54   *Page out of Mies van der Rohe, sketchbook 1925*

*2. **Resistance**.* In the definitions 'reach space' and 'cave space', the word 'space' is understood to be the opposite of substance or matter. Yet reach space presupposes the existence of matter, as for example the small water droplet suspended in the air whose restricted quantity expands into a snow crystal, since this type of material has the potential of unrestricted expansion in air. A cave space, however, comes into existence by means of expansion, just

35

55　J. PAXTON. Crystal Palace at Sydenham, 1851

56　MONIER & WAYSS. Road Bridge at Wildegg, 1880

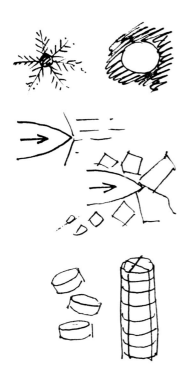

shopping firmly together. The example of the string bag, however, demonstrates something further, namely the presence of empty places between the various objects into which something else could still be put. Room for something signifies 'space'. This space can be enlarged by the appropriate re-arrangement of various objects. It will be noticed that the maximum space is obtained if we combine the objects into the form of a cross. If instead of the shopping we take two struts (which could consist of single elements held together) and cross them at right angles, and then instead of the string bag we take a rubber band and with it brace their ends to form a square with intersecting diagonals, we obtain a 'braced square' and also at the same time a basic model of a body. Two of these braced squares joined end to end result in a space which is entirely enclosed by rods or struts, i.e. the 'rod frame', made up of

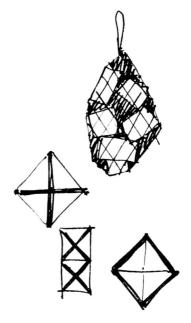

like a yeast bubble inside dough—here we are dealing with a pushing outwards and away of the surrounding matter.

Space and matter are relative concepts within the realm of substance: that is, space has the lesser resistance of the two substances, and can lose its form, whereas matter retains it. Thus the material 'boat' penetrates the space 'water'. The thing responsible for making the boat into a material is the elastic bond which links together all the individual nuclei which go to make up both the boat and the water. In just the same way an elastic band ties together a stack of draughts counters to form a single solid body, or a piece of paper wrapped round coins forms a solid roll, or a string bag holds the

the adjacent triangles of the braced squares. Thus we have a model for each type of case: the 'braced square' in terms of a body within space, and the 'rod frame' as a space inside the body. Incidentally these frames can be extremely economical and may be made up with a minimal outlay of material, as we can see in the example of the common circular wooden garden table and the deckchair.

stacked the shopping in the string bag in a vertical column. The ship's mast with its yard-arms is a braced square without the lower tension members, and so is a tent. These are all examples

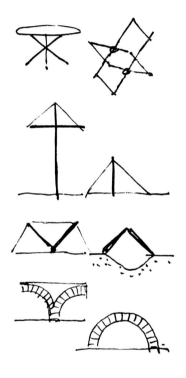

of 'reach space'. Conversely, the moat in the sand corresponds to the lower part of the surrounding rod framework. If it had a pitched roof of drift-wood, this would correspond to the upper part of a rod frame. Both the roof and the moat are 'recess' or 'cave' spaces.

All types of building construction can be shown to derive from the models described above. If for instance we multiply the arms in the braced square so that they become the spokes of a wheel or, even further, so that they close up and combine into a disk, then we obtain the cross-section of a sphere or of a medicine ball in which the stuffing

57 *AUGUST PERRET. Clothing factory, Paris 1919*
58 *FRANZ KRAUSE. Sketch design for a library, 1927*
59 *LUIGI NERVI. Stadium at Florence, 1930*
60 *Tubular steel chairs by Mart Stam and Mies van der Rohe, 1927*
61 *FRANK LI. WRIGHT. Falling Waters, 1936*
62 *MIES VAN DER ROHE. Office block, 1922*
63 *H. & B. RASCH. Project for a stadium with a suspended roof, 1928*
64 *H. & B RASCH. Suspended structures, flats, 1927*

When the force of gravity is applied to these two models, some of the tensile and compressive members will appear to exist already and will thus be redundant. In the case of the sand-castle, gravity replaces the tension of the rubber band, as it would if one

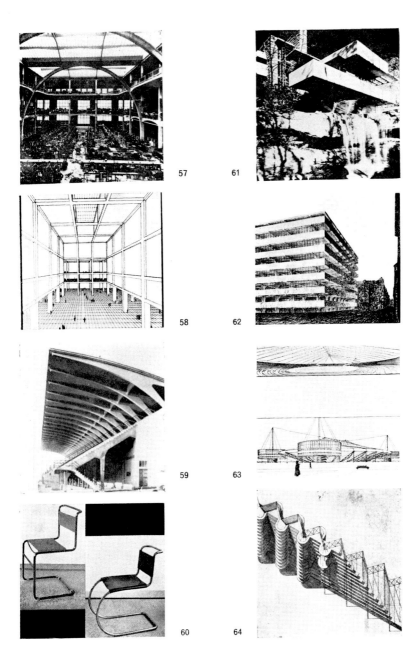

57

61

58

62

59

63

60

64

is pressing outwards against the leather skin: in other words, a solid body. Alternatively, if we multiply the diagonals of the rod frame so that they form a polygon held together by spokes, like the Big Wheel at the Prater in Vienna or the rim of a bicycle wheel, then we obtain the cross-section of a hollow sphere. This brings to mind Guerick's

of the sphere which is the important one: the upper half and the stuffing, when replaced by the force of gravity, become redundant, and we are left with a lower 'bowl' similar to a suspension roof, i.e. like the muslin cloth which a housewife suspends over a bowl to sieve flour. In the example of Guerick's Sphere the space is inside, and the lower half and the vacuum, replaced by the force of gravity, becomes redundant, leaving us with a cupola or dome.

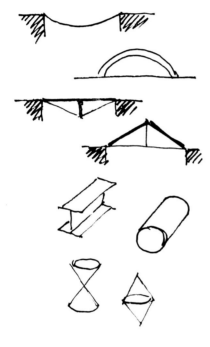

All suspension structures such as inverted trusses, vaults, and strut frames, are derived from the surrounding rod frame. Both the basic shapes, the braced square and the surrounding rod frame, can be converted into the third dimension in one of two ways: (1) through projection in depth, whereby the braced square could become converted into a profile girder and the surrounding rod frame into a tube; (2) through rotation about its own axis, whereby the braced square can become two cones joined at their vertices, and the surrounding rod frame a double cone. If one links such bodies together, then elements of the braced

Sphere, which consisted of two halves (it might just as easily consist of thousands of individual pieces) and from which the air was evacuated, so that the internal tie-rods are replaced by the pressure of the outside atmosphere. Each of these two hemispheres contains a roof structure. In the case of the medicine ball, where the space is exterior to the body, it is the lower half

square type result in a forest of columns and elements of the surrounding rod frame type interweave into a honeycomb structure. We can easily discover these prototypes in familiar building forms: in terms of resistance against gravity (floors), protection against rain (roofs), and against wind (walls). We find examples of the braced square vertically (like yard-arms) in a building with a suspended structure, horizontally in grandstands and aircraft hangars; vertical pipes in blocks of flats where walls are used as load-bearing members, and horizontal pipes in the tanked underground constructions commonly used nowadays. The 'forest of columns' corresponds to the uprights supporting the floors, as we see in examples of modern office blocks. We find the all-round, enclosed honeycomb in containers like those in which fuel is stored in ships and industrial plant.

41

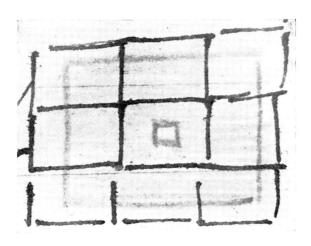

65   OSKAR SCHLEMMER. Sketch

3. Distance. If we add or subtract a portion of food on a plate we have created a spacial relationship between two separate bodies. If we cut a piece of cheese into slices, bars, or dice, this is a subdivision of one and the same body. In the first case, a body has been added; in the second case, a body has been subdivided. A landscaped garden is created by the addition of various objects, whereas an architectural garden is formed by the subdivision of the whole parterre. In the former there exists only two boundaries, in the latter one can have as many as one wants. In fact every space contains both types,

43

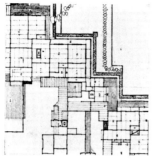

66 Plan of Katsura palace, Kyoto

67 Walls, partitions, etc., in the Katsura palace, Kyoto

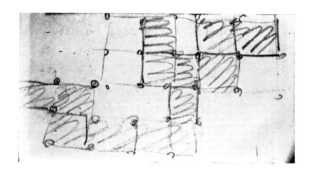

68 Page from author's sketch book, 1925

homogeneous relationship and signifies *interconnection*.

A waist-high counter top is connected to the floor by a base. We could also regard it as a table top of which the edge has been thickened by the height of the base. Our knees will find the base an obstruction if we wish to use the counter as a table to sit at and to

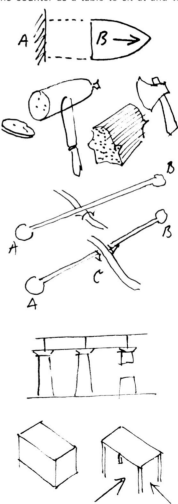

as we can see from our earlier example of the boat. As we push off from the shore we can measure the space between stern and shore; in other words we could divide this 'space between' with knife-cuts at right angles to the direction of movement, rather like slicing a salami; but we could also split it in the direction of movement, rather like splitting a log. But whereas each piece of 'firewood' split from this log maintains its own relationship between the shore and the boat, the first slice cut out of the salami instantly destroys its structural cohesion and hence the relationship between the two. The road connection between two towns **A** and **B** is interrupted if the bridge **C** is destroyed. The connection formed between ceiling and floor by a pillar is destroyed if one single layer of bricks is removed from the pillar—the ceiling must collapse. And so, as we have shown conclusively, the spatial relationship between two bodies can only be subdivided parallel to the direction in which they are related and not at right angles to it, because it is a

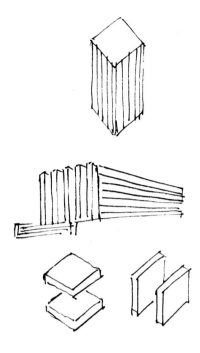

But these two categories of relationship must not become mixed up. In his lecture *External and Internal Walls* (Stuttgart, 1924), Eric Mendelsohn tried to define the difference between load-bearing members having a vertical relationship and the horizontal ones existing between interconnected planes. He described the external wall as a front, pierced, and forming the interconnecting link between inside and outside; on the other hand the internal wall was defined as being an intersection and horizontal dividing member between two similar interiors. The vertical category of interrelationships on the one hand (e.g. floor-ceiling) and the horizontal one on the other (e.g. walls) both belong to bodies; the cross-sections of the interrelated pairs are theoretically without substance (for example the pair of cleavage planes of a log split into two, being infinitely thin, could therefore be regarded to all intents and purposes as being without substance) and have to be evaluated as an opening, despite the interconnecting members contained within it such as supporting walls and props. If the interconnecting members are all drawn together to form one single column like the column of a hydraulic car lift then, apart from this column, there exists between the floor of the lift and the

put our knees underneath it. So enough material is taken away from the base to leave just enough for four table legs. Similarly the load-bearing walls of houses can be reduced to columns and pillars, whether we are speaking of temples, cathedrals, or even skyscrapers. The openings created in this way make it possible for horizontal relationships to exist such as we discussed in our previous example of the boat-shore relationship. The structural supporting members, belonging to the vertical category of floor-ceiling relationship, can however become connected at the perimeter boundaries with elements belonging to the horizontal category. Typical examples are the traditional brickwall type of construction or the long seats on the sides of trams, or again the fore and aft benches on pleasure boats.

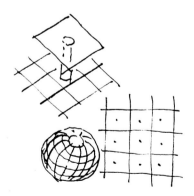

46

underside of the supporting platform only empty vacuum and the cleavage planes themselves which have no substance. Horizontally related systems can then extend unhindered in every direction within this free space. If we imagine this floor surface as being extended endlessly, interconnecting the related areas of many such bodies over the whole face of the earth, we would have an endlessly repeated dotted screen, a regular pattern over the whole surface. Now we are left with only an interior: the columns, or the bodies consisting of vertically related systems, lie completely within the screen surface and so must be very closely restricted in number and circumference.

Once again we can usefully demonstrate this with the example of a cube of cheese. The red wax rind separates the interior from the exterior and gives the body its cohesion. Let us call the six sides of the cheese cube its primary boundaries. If we cut one slice out of the middle, then this slice has only four external sides of rind, and two others which were formed by the cutting and which separate interior from interior. If one then cuts a strip out of the middle of the slice, one is left with only two exterior surfaces of rind by which this body can be held (for instance between thumb and middle finger), and with four cut planes. This would then constitute the model of a pair of related areas, irrespective of whether it is vertically or horizontally arranged. If we cut this strip again twice through the middle we obtain a cube consisting of nothing but interval planes formed by the cuts—we normally handle such a piece of cheese with a cocktail stick. Now returning to the last example but one when the cheese still had two exterior surfaces of rind, if we replace our fingers with a cocktail stick, we then have an example of two external or primary surfaces (the rind) being

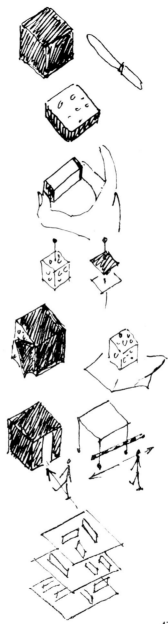

connected by a column—in other words the construction method of a mushroom roof. Once more, let us compare the original whole cheese enclosed by rind on all sides and the cut cube of cheese, open on all sides : in the former, the secondary action consists of breaking through the external wall, whereas in the latter it would be the closing of all openings. From this it follows that if (as in the former) one opens the sides, these openings will be vertical; and if (as in the latter) one closes the sides, these will be horizontally related areas.

Mies van der Rohe differentiated only between the vertical relation of ceiling and floor as being the primary system,

and the horizontal relation of the walls as forming the secondary system; in which case one must accept the primary system as being permanent and the secondary as being capable of change. In the case of the boat, the 'ceiling' becomes the water, with the tram it becomes the rails, and with the car it becomes the road. The vehicles are transformed into movable parts of the related planes because of their connection with them, rather like sliding doors, which are positioned in their direction of movement, in contrast to ordinary hinged doors, which penetrate into the room in a disrupting fashion when opened. Inevitably crossrelationships result where pairs of relationships are situated next to each other in such a way that their open sides become interconnected combined spaces, for example in the arrangement of corridor and compartments in a railway carriage. If we apply our principles properly we can find, or make up, just as many examples of this as we want.

This rather important chapter on walls has been difficult to illustrate because of its three-dimensional character, and the critical reader is asked to use his own judgment in filling out places where it lacked clarity, perhaps because the examples are too few or too imprecise.

48

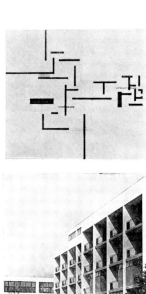

69

73

70

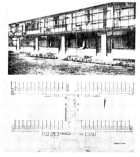

74

71

75

72

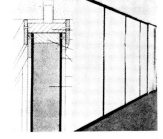

76

*77 H. & B. RASCH. Building with
adjustable wall, Stuttgart 1930 (exterior)*

*78 H. & B. RASCH. Building with
adjustable wall, Stuttgart 1930 (interior)*

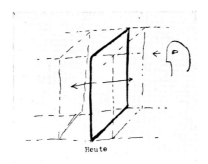

79 Drawing by Willi Baumeister concerning
the perception of a surface or plane

79a, b. WILLI BAUMEISTER. Interchangeable architecture

4. Perception. In trying to define what is a boundary and what an opening, we are frequently deceived.   What is a boundary for one of our senses may not be so for another. The shop window is actually a boundary, but to the eye it is an opening.   Fog is a boundary—but only to the eyes. Poison gas is also a boundary, but only for the respiratory organs.   There are as many types of space as man has senses. H. G. Wells described this well in his story about the country of the blind.   Dogs live almost completely in the world of smell, the bat almost entirely in the world of sound. So the decision as to what does,

51

80 WILL I BAUMEISTER. Drinking vessels in various materials, 1924

81 WILLI BAUMEISTER. Mural, 1924

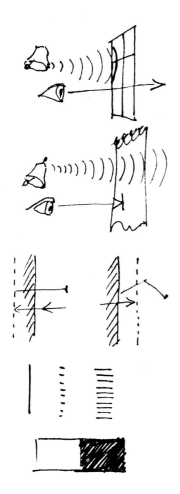

in this case the nail must be regarded as being the space. In this way we differentiate by means of our sense of touch between hard and soft, rough and smooth, just as the eye that recognises substance as light distinguishes between light and dark, and the ear between noise and silence. Contrast is the pre-requisite of perception. A state or condition is defined by comparison with its neighbouring state—for instance, in this place it is harder, there softer; here lighter, there darker; here louder, and there much quieter.

A space is characterised by a uniform state or condition. The change of this state determines its boundary. Perception of the change of state presupposes the existence of some form of motion. The sense of touch can only reach the immediately adjacent environment, for example by means of a stride. But the eye scans the whole field of vision in a fraction of a second because the whole of the retina is activated simultaneously. All objects in one's field of vision (for example one black dot or several dots) are perceived virtually simultaneously. However a black surface does not emit any light and therefore leaves the eye at rest; a

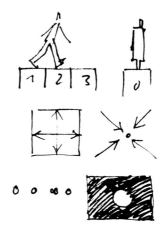

or does not, constitute a boundary must be a relative one. The sense of touch is used to judge according to the resistance encountered from a relative substance. We find this when we want to hammer a nail into a wall. If in so doing we encounter a gap, this is regarded as space. If the nail encounters a stone and bends, then it is as if this stone had entered into the domain of the nail, and

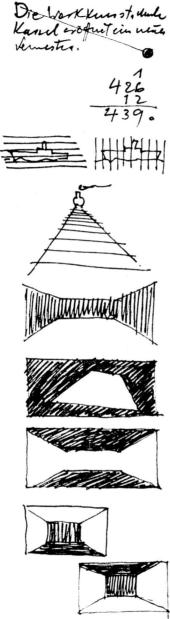

white dot on a black surface will only activate the central focusing area. And so in order to magnify the light source the eye needs to get closer: instead of just scanning over the surface, the eye is now making a definite motion towards it. This is the chief reason why black letters on a light background are more easily and quickly read than white letters on a black background—in the latter case the eye is forced to jump from one letter to the next. In scanning the surface the eye seeks first of all to perceive the most distant item within the relationship and only then scans what lies in between; as for instance when we read a letter we start at the point furthest away—the top left-hand corner—and proceed to the lower right-hand corner, and in adding up a column of figures the result is always found at the bottom right-hand corner, even though the figures are normally written from right to left during the adding-up process.

In the evaluation of spatial boundaries one's optical impressions are influenced by personal experiences of the sense of touch. For this reason, and because man's direction of movement is horizontal, we define a vertical articulation as being open and a horizontal one as being closed. Naturally one has to differentiate as to whether the observer is situated in the same space as the object he is looking at, that is if he is connected with it by

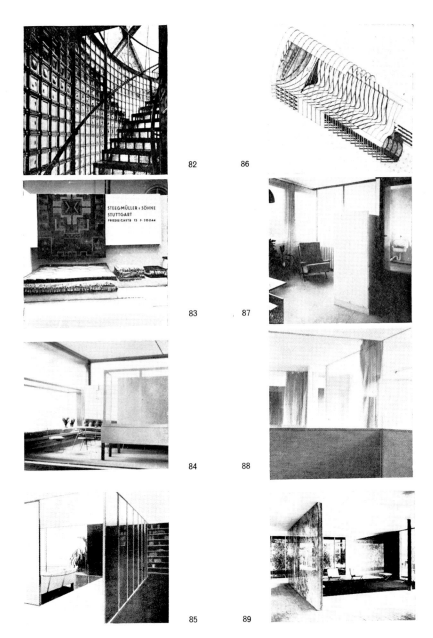

82

86

83

87

84

88

85

89

means of a plane of relationship such as a street or railway lines, or if what is really being dealt with is an isolated picture plane (such as a letter or a cinema screen or an ice rink) into which one mentally projects oneself. Such an isolation of the optical relationship may actually be desirable—as for instance with exhibition walls in museums which could perhaps be isolated merely by means of a black floor. Our conception of space is chiefly determined by the eye, and when evaluating its boundaries we interpret light and dark in terms of closed and open or near and far, and scan the scale of a space within the extent of the plane of relationship from right to left or vice versa.

Oskar Schlemmer pursued the problem of absolute space and considered that the task of the painter lay in making walls vanish. In 1938 he designed a rear wall for a staircase made up of dark blue, transparent, and vertically accentuated elements. In antithesis, his friend Willi Baumeister saw the painter's task as being the creation of objects—i.e. physical boundaries—and he did sketch designs for the side walls of the same staircase consisting of modulations in red and yellow, organised

plastically and accentuated horizontally. This is only one example of painters' ideas on the subject. One could study and examine in detail nearly everything in Mies van der Rohe's Barcelona Pavilion (1929), **89** which for this reason alone ought to be reconstructed as a specially important document of our century.

56

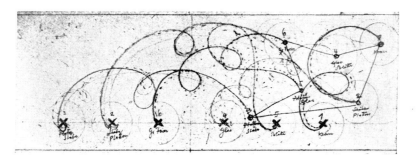

90 OSKAR SCHLEMMER. *Choreographic sketch*

5. *Path or route.* The architect was forced to come to terms with two phenomena in particular: the motor car and the conveyor belt. On the one hand man supplied himself with wheels which made him independent in the choice of his paths and aims, whereas on the other he allowed a mechanism to tie him down in place and time. However opposed these two new living components may seem, they have one thing in common—both look for the shortest connection between near and far objects. The manufacturer arranges working positions in the closest logical sequence. The shopkeeper puts his

*91   H. RASCH. Street with stepped-up
factory building, Wuppertal*

*92   FRANZ KRAUSE. Club House,
Wuppertal 1937*

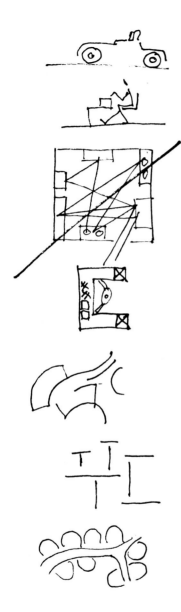

wares into the path of his customer in **95**
the way which will achieve the
quickest possible contact between the
two. After the First World War, when
because of social changes housewives
learned to manage without servants,
Bruno Taut adapted the method of
factory organisation to the planning of
houses, especially the kitchens. The
modern kitchen, saving time and
energy-wasting detours, is his major
work (*Woman as Creator*, 1924). Taut
tried to achieve the smallest circulation
space. Mies van der Rohe, on the
other hand, considered that everything
depended on a large coherent circulation space within which the various
objects (the rest positions) could be
placed in a generous spacial relationship
to each other. The same sense of purpose produced the city on piloti (1925)
and the multi-storey suspension structure city of 1927 where the buildings **103**
float above a free uninterrupted ground
surface entirely devoted to traffic. Here
was a differentiation between resting
space and motion space, between the
status quo and changing events—and
this was the true beginning of a theory
of space.

Along a river with its busy life lie
docks which are in a constant state of
repose. In London, and in Berlin, there
are suburbs with roadways carrying
only the through traffic, and from these
arteries other roads branch off leading
to the quiet cul-de-sacs of residential

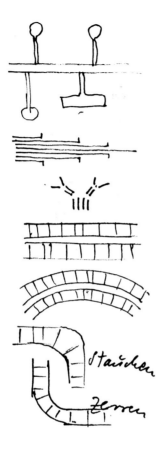

Rooms branching off on either side of the pathway or corridor can be assembled additively into chain-like wings, with the separating partition walls corresponding to the rungs of a ladder, or more precisely to the sleepers of a railway line. They are vertically related at right angles to the direction of motion of the traffic (i.e. the railway line) even when this is curved—when, in accordance with the principles of spatial geometry, the depth of the rooms is greater on the convex side than on the concave. The divergence of the walls in the case of a curved office block results on the convex side in a broadening out of the rooms towards the outside face of the building, and on the concave side the rooms widen out towards the corridor (i.e. the interior of the building). In this way the sharply angled form of the room affects the traffic route. Internal objects such as the furniture are not affected. It is possible to position them at right angles to the side walls and they can even form room dividers.

If the chain of rooms is curved far enough to become an enclosed ring, then we have achieved a circular building in which the concave side forms the core, the circulation area being central. The circular building is therefore the prototype of the point block or skyscraper. Such a building consists of an entirely enclosed mass, its form being largely determined by external forces,

48 developments. In contrast to Mies van der Rohe, Hugo Haering made the traffic arteries the basis of the floor plans of his dwellings. The rooms open onto the corridor like tributaries into a river and allow it to broaden towards the exit. Conversely the traffic is distributed like the branches of a tree to the last little room cells. In this way the central and additive ground-plan is evolved, as in the landscape garden mentioned earlier; and as in this garden, we have curvilinear paths, since a body once set in motion tends to avoid sharp corners.

93 H. RASCH. Shadowless junction of ceilings, walls and columns, 1947
94 H. RASCH. House-plan in form of circulation routes
95 American department stores, 1946
96 FRANZ KRAUSE. Floor plans with 'cells' and living spaces
97 H. RASCH. Plan with 'deep' interior
98 H. RASCH. House with 'deep' plan, 1955
99 GINSBURG. 1½ height interlocking maisonettes with corridors, 1929
100 LE CORBUSIER. Unité d'Habitation at Marseilles, 1952 (same concept as that by Ginsburg)

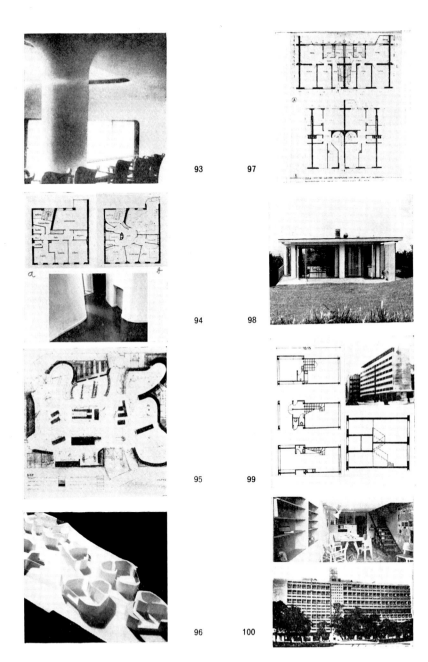

93

97

94

98

95

99

96

100

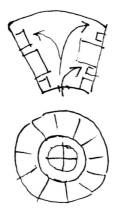

multiplied and is thus an infinite and unrestricted form. That which is totally enclosed radiates outwards from a central point and this remains valid whether it is one unit or many. A single unit can touch several objects in a quite random sequence, in other words relating them back centrally to itself; many units, if they do not wish to interfere with one another, must move past the object in one direction only, rather as in a one-way street, in which case the number of objects is finite and limited and they close up into a circle. In order to get into and out of this circle the objects must be linked to the centre in some fashion, i.e. they must be interlinked and combined to form an island. 'Islands within a space filled

for example sun, air, aspect, circulation, traffic, etc.—one example being the lighthouse, which has a circular shape offering the least area of resistance to the wind and other elements, or the ship, whose shape is determined by resistance to water currents.

Taut and Haering had envisaged such a 'machine for living in' as an enclosed mass with its own conclusive shape like the house of a snail. The house thus becomes a 'tool' like a spoon, cup, handle or chair. All these tools stand in the same relationship to their equivalent bodies as does the matrix to the patrix. In this instance we are thinking not so much of what is understood by individual form—the individual is firmly combined with the lifespan of an object such as a tailor-made suit—but rather of finite and complete circular forms like the pebble completely ground down into a rounded end product by the action of the stream. The circle is the form representing motion; the rectangle is a static form. The circle is a form within a space, but the rectangle is the space itself. The circle is a finite and restricted form; the rectangle on the other hand can be divided and

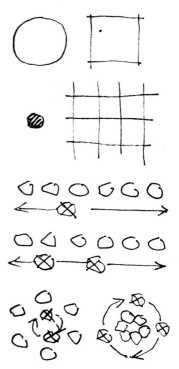

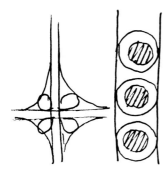

with traffic and movement' were the subject of Willi Baumeister's writing and painting. Such islands can be joined together to form so-called 'island chains'. Quite different from this is the theoretically unlimited criss-cross grid pattern of the traditional blocks of buildings in examples of modern town planning where the traffic is interrupted at each cross section. This pattern makes traffic rules a necessity, as Oskar Schlemmer demonstrated in his ballet in 1925. The fusion of both

schemes led to a ribbon development 90 planning principle: the island chains are bridged over by elevated highways and connected with the main road system by clover leaf systems at the intersection points. Sketch schemes for such ribbon developments were evolved in the late 'twenties, but a well-known architectural magazine refused to publish them in 1954, saying this was 'outmoded Americanism'. 108

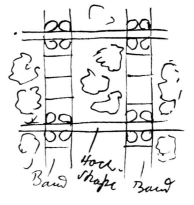

CONCLUSION

Following the publication of the book *How to Build* in 1927, Bruno Taut called for a 'Technology of space'. So far we haven't found one, so we shall have to be content for the moment with these observations on the elements of space. This is mainly a retrospective view of years of search and trial and error in the attempt to test the truth of things which had merely been quickly sketched in outline. In the twenty-five to forty years which have gone by, architects have mainly been engaged in

the solution of practical problems. But there is not one of them who did not profit from the discoveries in architectural theory made in the 'twenties. Shall we be satisfied and let the matter rest here, or shall we explore a little further? We hope our observations will have shown that the phenomenon of space is still full of unsolved questions, and that the answers to these should illuminate and enrich the practice of architecture.

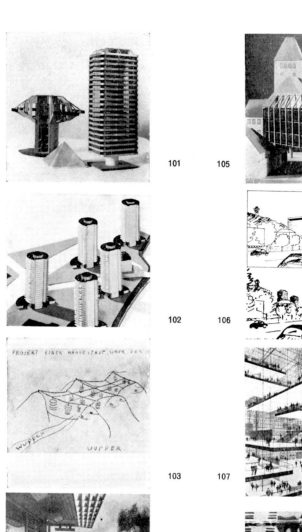

101

102

PROJEKT EINER HANGESTADT UBER DER

WUPPER.   WUPPER.

103

104

105

106

107

108

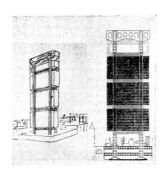

109 A. WILLIAMS. Building with
suspended structure, project 1944

101 H. RASCH. Model of a block of flats with
suspended structure, 1955
102 H. RASCH. Buildings with suspended
structures, 1955
103 FRANZ KRAUSE. Suspended city over
the River Wupper, 1943
104 Pedestrian precincts at Linda Vista,
California, USA
105 H. RASCH. Building with suspended
structure, over a roadway, 1955

106 MART STAM. Suspended slab blocks,
above a road, 1956 (alternative proposal for
project of point blocks with suspended structure,
1955)
107 CONRAD LEHMANN. Suspended slabs
and planes, sketch design, 1956
108 H. RASCH. 'Linear' city with industrial,
commercial and civic islands. Chains and
dwelling zones linked with high-level avenues of
traffic

65

3. THE MASTERY OF TECHNOLOGY

Lecture given to the Debating Forum at Kassel on 22nd and 23rd November 1964

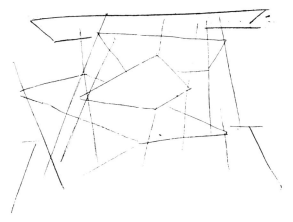

110   WILLI BAUMEISTER. Sketch

The house, piece of furniture and tool which is specially designed, make up, nowadays, only a small fraction of our daily requirements and their numbers are steadily dwindling. We might sincerely regret this trend: catering for the individual is quite rightly asserted to be a personal necessity, and many people would like to escape from this ocean of mass production onto any quiet islands which may still exist. However one cannot fail to recognise the fact that our principal 'chattels', apart from a few exceptions, consist of mass-produced articles, i.e. standard-ised reproductions. The people who

*111–112 Sketch design by author for a block
of flats with suspended structure, 1964*

68

produce these articles have long since ceased to be craftsmen; and this change is apparent even in the name given to the various training institutes which, originally known as The Royal Arts and Crafts Trade College, and later on called The Training College for German Craftsmen, then altered to The School for Working Arts. The specially coined term 'Working Arts' is ambiguous, but we are still aware of the climate of thought which for the past forty years prevented the use of the much more correct word *gestaltung* (creative design). Nevertheless we think we know that we are dealing here, not with cottage industries for arts and crafts shops, but with samples and prototypes for industrial mass-production.

What does the word *gestaltung* mean? Creative design, or more precisely the act of creation, has its beginning in the simultaneous apperception of varied concepts. First of all there is the full exploitation of materials and working methods, whereby the main importance lies chiefly in what one understands by the term 'workmanlike' or 'rightness' in the making of something, that is, the full tactile and visual appreciation of the qualities of both the material and the tool. Then there is the 'functional form', in which the correct functioning of the relationship between two objects is all important (in the case of a doorknob or a chair one of the two objects concerned can be the person himself). The functional form is at first largely an abstract product of the imagination, a phantom without material substance; its realisation is then a second act of creation. The introduction of materials and structures into abstract concepts of form inevitably means an act of compromise, and the phrase 'Architecture is the art of feasibility' therefore contains a sense of resignation to this state of affairs.

Function and technology must combine in such a way as to reduce to a minimum those portions of problems which remain unsolved and limited by compromise, so that one does not feel them to be annoying obstacles. For technology will only be mastered when objects and tools, rooms and spaces and developments, are composed in such a way that *we no longer have to look after them*, that is, so that their inherent problems no longer invade our consciousness—as is, for example, already the case with the electric light switch and the telephone. *To the degree that we are still concerned with technology, it has not yet been mastered;* and to that degree it will cause discomfort, for the sector of technology over which we have not yet attained mastery harbours many risks and is more or less an adventure—as for example wave research and space craft are today. We can easily demonstrate this by means of two examples: first the timber chair of 1924, machine-made within an assured timber technology of circular saw and spindle drill, allows the omission of an adequate reference to its user (and one could quote Morgenstern at this point, also the famous chair by Rietfeld of 1924); on the other hand, the futuristic pictures of a city which appeared in 1924, and the architectural model by Finsterlin which came out at the same time, are rendered completely unrealistic and absurd by a lack of sufficient technology.

Technology encompasses many things of short and of long duration, the latter being building developments which serve both as shelter and for change of location, that is, spaces devoted to residential and transport needs. The durability of these building developments forces one over and over again into the position of having to fashion other objects and functions to fit in with them. We are fully aware of what accompanying problems this sort of thing brings, for instance when a large apartment or factory is suddenly

50

divided into two smaller ones or vice versa, and also when roads and parking spaces, built only a few years ago, are suddenly no longer sufficient. In 1925, in the magazine 'Baugilde' an article appeared entitled *We are Building Ruins* which advocated the development of internal and external walls and houses in such a way that they would adapt to rapidly altering requirements, saying that for this reason they should be light and mobile, while the structural floors, being the only permanent element, should be strong and load bearing, free as far as possible from vertical supports and columns, and with evenly distributed lighting and air-conditioning, so that they became multi-purpose. This sort of approach was the basis of the early projects of Mies van der Rohe and Mart Stamm; mobile walls were demonstrated for the first time in the

84, 85, 119 apartment of the Weissenhofsiedlung and, two years later, a house was built at Stuttgart-Botnang having mobile internal and external wall panels of uniform size and universal interchangeability which has remained unaltered to the present day, apart from the alterations arising from the interchanges of the wall panels. The basic principle and indeed the pre-requisite for this is a grid or module, as for instance in the

66, 67 case of the traditional Japanese house; and, as is well known, this system has become highly significant in the sphere of office and store design. But this is not the only possibility. There is also another which was already hinted at in the 1920s in the form of projects: the creation of prefabricated *assembly or heart units* (Krause called them 'kiosks')

96 —bathroom units, kitchen units, bedroom units, etc.—whereby the outside wall between the floors is kept open, or rather is only protected from the elements by large panes of glass. It is freely admitted, of course, that in this respect planning and technology are still in the kindergarten stage, but when one considers that today whole car

bodies are moulded in plastic one must ask oneself, 'Why not a whole bathroom, or a kitchen, or a workspace?' With such a system the floor plan would to a large extent become free from the limitations of a grid or other confining boundaries; and then, providing the resultant acoustic problems can be solved, internal walls become entirely superfluous, as for example can be seen in large offices, for instance Bertelsmann at Gütersloh. Just think how many dust-traps and corners disappear!

Whether we are dealing here with walls or units does not matter. In either case we are no longer concerned with the various components of the building in the traditional sense of the word. This type of building could be created entirely without them and would look just the same however they are placed or whether they are there or not. Mies van der Rohe therefore included all these elements (I use the word 'elements' here to avoid the misleading term 'component') in the concept 'secondary system', in contradistinction to the permanent structural floor slabs and vertical columns, which he called the 'primary system'. This 'primary system' is especially significant because it is wholly neutral in relationship to its use: the ground floor may be part of the street, contain shops or

113 New York, aerial photograph
114 BREUGHEL. Tower of Babel
115 H. & B. RASCH. Structural skeleton of a building in Stuttgart, 1930
116 FRANZ KRAUSE. Linear housing scheme Haselhorst, Berlin 1929
117 Imaginary picture of a city of the future, 1925
118 FRANK LI. WRIGHT. Mile-high centre skyscraper
119 FRANZ KRAUSE & H. RASCH. Interchangeable partitions, 1938
120 H. RASCH. Housing development, 1954

113

117

114

118

115

119

116

120

garages; the upper floors can be used for offices or flats. Here we are really concerned with nothing other than the multiplication of the ground surface, which has become too scarce, and on which the 'secondary' walls or units are erected just as if we were dealing with single-storey buildings lacking only the roof—indeed a strong impetus came from the prefabricated elements of factory-made bungalows, in which the wall panels, bathroom units, and services units could quite often be assembled without any need for floor slabs or structure. Even if the prefabricated house (and the caravan and camping grounds also belong in this category) cannot be exactly co-ordinated in terms of a secondary system, we nevertheless find ourselves in a border-line area which is a pointer to totally new possibilities for ways of living and dwelling. Here there is a complete break with the ancient concept of the room as the basic element of architecture: and from this juncture new ways open up for the improved accommodation of the masses of humanity in terms of four, or even forty, storeys in the big cities.

So much for the secondary system. The floors or levels themselves are defined in terms of primary systems. They are the permanent and unalterable elements, and form the main picture of the city. For this reason, Mies demands that they should also be made visible and be fully expressed by the architect. 'I want to *see* the primary element,' he lectures. But one may wonder whether, behind all this, there lies not a trace of the old classicism of Peter Behrens. It has never been finally established whether or not it is really desirable to use the columns and floor slabs of the structural framework of a house as a means of its artistic expression. How often have columns not been found to be disruptive elements inside a department store, factory, office, or living room, if only for the simple reason that they get in the way. In the battle with beauty, the right practice is usually that which functions in terms of steel and reinforced concrete whose possibilities we are slowly beginning to understand. We marvel just how far floor slabs are capable of spanning and how large the distances between structural columns can be, and just how slim these columns can be made; but their true inherent possibilities are only finally revealed in cantilever and suspension structures. One thinks at this point of the cantilever chair by **60** Mart Stamm, and the huge roof structures which float, apparently without support, above the enormous grandstands of sports stadia; one remembers also the floor slabs which (as in the buildings of Frank Lloyd Wright) soar **61** out above precipices far into the air and so achieve that feeling of hovering in space which previously the architect only managed to simulate by illusionary means such as covering the columns with mirrors or using many closely-spaced, thin cast-iron supports.

With cantilever structures, if only because of the indivisibility of their overall form and the large extent of their mass, the limitless interrelationship

---

121 *LE CORBUSIER. Plans of the Unité d'Habitation, Marseilles*
122 *H. RASCH. Fan-shaped layers and compartments in a block of flats, 1947*
123 *FRANK Ll. WRIGHT. Sturges house in California, 1939*
124 *FRANK Ll. WRIGHT. Johnsons wax factory, 1944*
125 *H. RASCH. Block of flats, 1947*
126 *PETER BEHRENS. Terraces and roof garden*
127 *H. RASCH. Roof-top restaurant and helicopter landing platform, Essen 1963*
128 *H. RASCH. Hospital project with suspended structure, 1965*

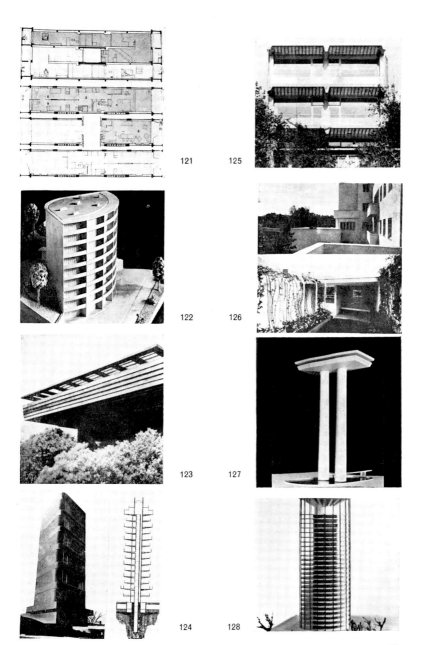

121

125

122

126

123

127

124

128

73

with the grid is abandoned. Up to this point we had covered all surfaces with a grid similar to the lines of latitude and longitude in geography and believed that in this way we had mastered everything quantitatively, in the firm belief that we had found the final solution for all time. Now, however, in place of the *divisive system* of densely chequered co-ordinates, we have these easily understood, finite surfaces, strung together in island chains, stratified in groups, fitted into each other like leaves, all combining into an *additive system*. The empty space surrounding these islands has now become the essential point of interest for the town planner and inhabitant alike: it is precisely this interconnecting space which forms the link with the nearest island, as also with the furthest one, and everybody is, by means of this space, linked with every other island. This results in a new and different concept of the world. It is as though everything has become separated into small lumps like the curd in sour milk: 'All particles have become separate from each other and are freely suspended in a plane or in space.'

These words were not written by an architect but by the painter Willi Baumeister, whose pictures in his later period mainly show island-like formations where the linking space between the islands gains a special significance —Baumeister calls it 'the negative'. Essentially this is precisely the same as in architecture, or as in our modern cosmologically-determined idea of the universe. And thus a spatial order becomes understandable with which modern town planning is concerned: the so-called 'island and ribbon town system' where the inhabitants are concentrated as pedestrians and the traffic is diverted round the outside, with cul-de-sacs which reach into the interior of the island, rather as into a dockyard. By this means man has

managed to break out into the distances of total space, completely decentralised and outward-orientated—to escape from the cell-like space, with its unending boxed-in walls. Mankind has become possessed by a totality with which nature is interreleated—which indeed in the final analysis is nature itself, since in any case all the artificially created and added pieces of architecture, surfaces, islands, spaces, etc., are completely absorbed by nature.

In his unpublished work *Modulation and Patina*, Baumeister says 'In an artistically creative activity, just as with the very stuff of which the whole universe is made, the only important thing is the transformation of surfaces in terms of thinness or thickness, roughness or smoothness, light or dark, etc., which one calls *modulation*'. One should also listen to Krause who, together with Baumeister, made several practical experiments in this respect.

These were entirely organisational and technical aspects of painting however.

But where, you will wonder, does this leave architecture? I believe that anyone who thinks and creates in the way we have described, or who in this way is trying to achieve the future with all the inherent problems which must be solved if humanity is to be protected from catastrophy, will find problems of aesthetics of little or no concern. Aesthetics exists or not, all depending on whether or not the problem has been correctly solved. But one doesn't have

---

129 Unesco building, Paris 1952
130 Highway intersection at Los Angeles, USA
131 FRANZ KRAUSE. Garden pond
132 Suspended roof structures
133 LE CORBUSIER. Block of flats standing in a park
134 H. RASCH. Systems of dwelling islands, 1953
135 FRANZ KRAUSE. Plan of a private house, 1963
136 H. & B. RASCH. Suspended roof, 1927

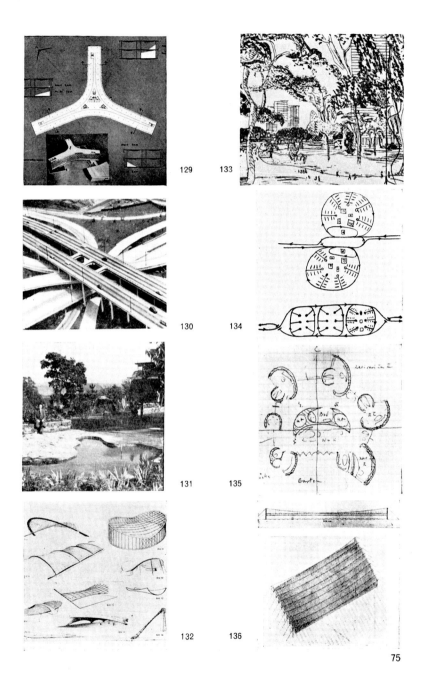

129

130

131

132

133

134

135

136

to worry about aesthetics—it occurs to excess in the modes of the time, in fashion, even, for all I care, in new styles of architecture. All the new elements which arouse the bewilderment and amazement and interest of the masses rush upon us in the form of a modern 'cosmetic', which then becomes a cheap and common medium with which to satisfy and flatter the mania of the masses for modernity. Unfortunately this cosmetic, like all aesthetics, is also the birthplace of lies, illusions, and fraud. Everything which is not solved and is waiting impatiently for a solution is transformed by means of aesthetics into a condition where it appears as though everything were perfectly all right. Aesthetics prevents a look at the real underlying problems, lies about the weaknesses, obstructs the road to discovery, development, and understanding; and for this reason I must acknowledge myself to be the firm opponent of aesthetics and of all 'beauty treatments'. I am sorry, but even in architecture only one thing should really have any value: the search for truth. By means of aesthetics, technology can never be mastered. Not even beauty! And, misquoting Wilhelm Busch:

What's beautiful (a fact I know)
Is when you've let aesthetics go.

TO SUMMARISE ON THE ABOVE CHAPTER

Lecture given at the School for Textile Engineering, Krefeld, on 15th February 1960

By the mastery of technology I mean the creation of tools, spaces, and machinery which are fashioned in such a way, and which we know so well how to handle, that we do not have to look after them in any way and that their inherent problems are excluded from our consciousness: as for example with the electric light switch or the telephone. To the degree that technology keeps us occupied, to that degree we have not mastered it; and to that degree it will give us problems, since unmastered technology contains inherent unpredictabilities and is more like an adventure, as for instance today the research into rays and space craft.

Technology encompasses many things, both short-lived and long-lived. The long-lived ones are building enterprises serving on the one hand as accommodation and on the other for change of scene—in other words, the spaces in which we stay, and those in which we travel. The durability of these building enterprises forces us always to fit everything else and every other function to them. That is why this question is so very important: to what extent has technology been mastered here and now, and how far does it remain unmastered?

1. THE TOWER OF BABEL—MILE-HIGH SKYSCRAPER. The Tower of Babel stands as a symbol of unmastered technology. The structure, shown in this picture by the painter Breugel, we unfortunately, and quite unthinkingly, take on trust in exactly the same way as we believe in the Mile-High Tower of

11◄
11▲

Babel by the architect Frank Lloyd Wright—because we know of the existence of the Eiffel Tower and the Empire State Building. What is it that has not been mastered in this instance? It is the huge increase of population, the mass of people which collects in these gigantic towers of flats, rather as in castle forecourts during the Middle Ages when people took refuge before a local battle.

17 2. CITY OF THE FUTURE—TERMITE HILL. But even this picture of a future metropolis, dating from the early 1920s, does not give the impression of a mastered technology even though in this case all the latest technological advancements have been utilised. Comparison with a termite hill is inescapable. Technology sprang up in the last century, with its growing industrial population and all its inherent social problems. The architect was completely at a loss as to how to cope with masses of workers and methods of mass transport. These were anti-cultural and ugly by-products of civilisation, lacking any significance in terms of his understanding of architecture.

3. COLUMN, VAULT—FAÇADE, ROOFS. By this the architect understood the status-imposing façade and proud pediments and turrets. What use had he for a technology which maintained that, out of four of the columns in his design, at least two were superfluous when the stone lintel was replaced by a steel beam? Or that five cross-vaults could be omitted and replaced by a flat slab of reinforced concrete?

40 4. GROSBERG HANOVER—STOCKHOLM. This type of architecture last found its expression during the Gothic period and the Renaissance; and our predecessors of two generations ago virtually needed only to differentiate between these two styles and then just to 'clothe' all remaining building elements and tools with the corresponding type of ornament. The last generation developed these motifs and styles still further by including the museum pieces of all historical periods and races.

5. FISCHER — SCHMITTHENNER· These both became deeply immersed in our cultural heritage. They learned with increasing skill to imitate the images of their germanic past, and to disguise radiators with stylistically accurate wrought-iron grilles and electric light bulbs with candelabra. In spite of all this they succeeded only in achieving a two-dimensional stage-set instead of a three-dimensional space.

6. BÖCKLINS TOTENINSEL—VAN GOGH. And—as is usual in this topsy-turvy world—artists of that same period were particularly concerned with representation of the third dimension. This sort of thing was already known during the time of Pompeii, particularly as used in the optical expansion of rooms, and appeared in the perspectives on theatrical back-cloths. In fact the paintings of two generations ago, with their heavy gilt frames, were really like stage sets, whether they depicted scenes from everyday life, or history, or landscapes. Yet it was these painters who first (and long before the architects) rediscovered the 'elementary principles', as Baumeister calls them. Quite uninfluenced by Oriental ink paintings, they discovered that the field of vision consists of shapes and colours, placed one next to the other and not one behind the other, and they were now engaged in bringing the image forward, from its spatial depth, onto the picture plane.

7. JUGENDSTIL—GAUDI. And now a very peculiar thing happened: it was the painters who made the first breach in the jealously guarded traditionalism of architecture, by attempting to express on façades the internal spaces hidden behind the elevations (for example Van de Velde, Behrens, Gaudi). These architect-painters even attempted to take various motifs from modern tech-

nology. Although this resulted in somewhat clumsy conjuring tricks, these nevertheless did expose something which up to that time no one had wanted to admit; and this exposure, a disquieting one to say the least, was of technology—the great unknown which one didn't really know how to cope with. One became rather frightened.

8. ROHLFS—BEDROOM. This fear found expression in paintings. The motifs, distorted into triangles or squares, are transformed into symbolic shapes, and the result is a flat, tapestry-like pictorial idiom. Though these pictures form a lasting record of their time and environment, this is not so in the case of consumer goods such as bedroom furniture, where one is concerned only with the technological resources of the time which are subject to rapid change.

29   9. WYLERBERG—DUDOK. The architect, who in his despair sought a way out, now became of the opinion that a *plastic* architecture should equate with this type of painting—a form structure similar to crystalline formations. Was not the crystal, in a larger sense, also related to technology? Was it therefore not possible by this means to catch technology out—that is, to outwit it? So now one attempted to build up architecture in terms of pyramids and cubes.   But the crystal formations forced one into even worse violations of floor plans than did the distorted façades.

46   10. TAUT—DÖCKER.   Behind the imposing façades stood the unadorned structure of the building. Therefore the first and most important thing one had to do was to strip houses of their façades rather like stripping an animal of its pelt. In 1924 Bruno Taut advised housewives to saw the decoration off their furniture—a process which has since become known as *tauten*. It was most important to express the extent of a space and even every object in it in as precise and bare a fashion as

possible.   But the forces and motions also had to be expressed; and for this purpose the new building material, concrete, was the most suitable.

11. KANOLD—BAUMEISTER.   In a similar way, the painters attempted to substitute the actual for the apparent. Thus there came about an objective representation of the material world, free from all accidents of mood or lighting as well as from the individual character of brush-strokes, which began as a new reality and later ended with the demise of surrealism.

At this point we have left that era which has been assessed as the final offshoot of historic eclectic architecture—an era in which Spengler was not alone in thinking he saw the decline of the West, and in which the first steps were taken towards a new architecture.

12. CRYSTAL PALACE— MONIER **55, 5**
BRIDGE. The bases of the new architecture, however, rest further back. People were simply unable to recognise them as such.   They were the iron, steel, and reinforced concrete structures of the nineteenth century, especially important examples of which are Paxton's Crystal Palace in London (1851), and the reinforced concrete bridge, spanning 39 metres, built in the 1880s in Wildegg by Wayss in accordance with Monier's patent of 1873. Both the designers, Paxton and Monier, were neither architects nor painters— they were gardeners!

13. ELEVATED RAILWAY IN NEW YORK—UNDERGROUND RAILWAY IN LONDON. And from approximately the same period come the beginnings of elevated and underground railways. These are modes of mass transport separated from the roads and relegated to different planes, signifying nothing less than the discovery of a third dimension for the transport space—a concept which has become quite familiar to us today in terms of the big motorway systems.   This picture shows the first elevated railway in New York, built in

the 1880s, and the London Tube trains, which go back to 1860. Berlin's Stadtbalm, going back to the 1870s, should also be mentioned here.

14. SCHEME—SCHEME. Space was now seen in terms of empty floor surfaces and unlimited storeys, reminiscent of the wall shafts of the burnt-out shells of blocks of flats and the concrete floors of burnt-out office blocks. The parts which survived, namely the walls in the one and the floors in the other, were the primary systems. The burned timber floors and roofs in the shafts of the blocks of flats, and the walls in the office blocks, were the secondary systems. The primary system of the vertical brick structure had been supplanted by the primary system of the horizontal steel frame and reinforced concrete structure.

5, 6 15. MENDELSOHN—MIES POINT BLOCK. The new house consisted of an extended horizontal plane. In the example of Mendelsohn's office block, the windows have been entirely replaced by a continuous horizontal opening—i.e. an endless horizontal slot. In the point block design by Mies van der Rohe, windows as such no longer exist but are entirely replaced by glass curtain walling.

55 16. DRINKING VESSEL — GLASS PALACE. The new building techniques put an end to the exciting contrast between wall and window which formed the main significance of traditional architecture, and in its place was put a wall surface which, as in the case of a drinking vessel, could consist of metal, timber, earthenware, or glass. Naturally it should consist of glass if at all possible, so that the primary architectural system, i.e. the horizontal floors, become visible.

86 17. GLASHAUS, COLOGNE—SWIMMING BATHS. But in the final analysis, wasn't glass a building material, like any other? The glass house in Cologne by Bruno Taut was erected in memory of the poet Paul Scheerbart, who in his novels and poems promoted the idea of buildings of glass, for example: 'Light pervades everything and comes alive as in a crystal. Without a palace of glass life is a burden. In the house of glass there is no fire, there is no need for a fire brigade . . .' Is it then so surprising that even a huge indoor swimming bath with a glass pool was designed? Just think: how about diving into a huge crystal bowl! This design was originated in 1927.

18. KANDINSKI—SCHWITTERS. Also even the painters freed themselves from the constraint of the vanishing point of perspective, and we see signs of this in respect of the picture plane. Content totally disappears in favour of pure form and colour experiences which are to be regarded as relationships within the plane. Finally it results in a transformation of the picture plane into either a materialised or a dematerialised one.

19. PARISIAN FACTORY — BARCELONA PAVILION. Because of the glass curtain wall, the functional separations of the bearing and separating building elements became visible. Walls are barriers against the unwelcome attacks of the elements—wetness, heat, cold, wind, smells, noise, and moving objects. All these attacks can be repelled by means of a pane of glass, and for screening from light and vision a curtain of suitable thickness is quite sufficient. The primary and secondary systems are often fully apparent: the skeleton, that is the columns and flat slabs serving as unalterable primary elements of the structure, and the independently changeable walls which can be adjusted to any particular requirement. In this picture of Perret's factory in Paris one can see the delicate structural frame which floats above the glass roof; and in Mies van der Rohe's Barcelona pavilion the cruciform columns (faced with chromium-plated metal sheeting) carry the roof slab and **57, 89**

clearly demonstrate that the glass and marble walls are merely self-supporting and not load-bearing in any way.

85, 77 20. GLASS WALLS—WEIßENHOF: WALLS. The secondary wall elements, however, had to be capable of mass-production in the same way as furniture. One had to be able to demount them into separate parts, individual slabs, and reassemble these again; also one had to be able to arrange these slabs as necessary to act as barriers against heat, cold, or noise. Then, in order to make mass-production feasible, there was still the factor of the size of the wall slabs and the finding of a uniform system which satisfied every case—and this gave rise to the screen.

66, 67 21. EMPEROR'S PALACE, JAPAN— WALLS. The factors listed above remind one very much of Japanese architecture. These buildings are also based on a kind of screen pattern: the measure of the living space is the mat. In 1927 we felt very close to the goal of regarding houses as fabricated mass-articles, that is, as mass-produced products. We had learned to give particular preference to reproduction: there was no rival to standardisation and the repetition it led to was popular. One has only to think about washing machines, typewriters, telephones, and cooking stoves.

22. HOUSE REINHARDT—WALLS. The less noticeable any participation of the individual is in mass-production, the 77, 78 more that mass-production seems genuine: as for instance in the example of the grid house, the Reinhardt House built in Stuttgart in 1929-30 with prefabricated and alterable external and internal walls and roof slabs, which has not been surpassed to this day.

23. STUTTGART MARKET — HEB-MÜLLER. The grid façade kept the promise made by its discoverers and promoters. It can be applied without alteration to dwellings and factories. In this example the grid forms the inexorable basis which cannot be dis-arranged or influenced by any constructional element, as can be seen in this illustration of the Power Station at Wulfrath. What stands out is not the construction, but the system.

24. BLOCK OF FLATS BY MIES— POINT BLOCK, ZEILEN. The universality of this principle, that is its general applicability, led to linear building. This 71, began in the Karlsruhe-Dammerstock Competition at which Mies van der Rohe, as judge, decided in favour of the North/South linear design of Häsler, the architect from Celle. The bands were placed, independently of streets and of the form of the site, at equal distances and running exactly North/South, giving all the flats identical daylight conditions. This fulfilled a social demand. A year later the East/West linear type was added, in the form of the arcade house in which the living rooms were orientated only to the South, and on the North side were placed access balconies, staircases, and service rooms such as bath and kitchen. This picture shows the linear block of flats of the Weißenhofsiedlung by Mies van der Rohe; and, next to it, a linear point block project by Gropius from the year 1930.

25. SET BACK GROUND-FLOOR PLAN—ANTWERP. If the floor slabs are to be continuous and uninterrupted bands, then one has to get rid of all the vertical breaks of staircase towers. This led to the transfer of staircases and toilets into the inside of the buildings, and in turn to the recessed ground-floor plan. The recessed ground-floor plan was notable because its frontage was shorter than the normal linear element by about a third. This meant that roads, too, were one-third shorter and that there was one-third more open area. This sort of thing was already familiar here in Antwerp 300 years ago when the recessed ground plan was used in merchants' houses where the façades were almost completely lost in the fenestration.

100 26. GINSBURG—CORBUSIER. The most interesting examples of the recessed ground floor arose through the substitution of tiered ramps for the vertical staircase shafts. Towards the end of the 1920s this type of design was realised in Ginsburg's house at Rostokino in Russia. Twenty years later Corbusier built his colossus at Marseilles, with its 24-metre long flats, in the same manner.

122 27. THE FAN SHAPE—PROBST. A further version of the recessed ground floor is the fan shape, which can be thought of as being brought about by drawing arcades together. In all recessed ground-floor plans, opening up the outer wall completely is a valid solution, as the outsize window is no longer a waste, any more than are balconies extending the whole width of the building.

28. BREUER—BREUER. In the ideal example, windows extend the full height of the wall so that the house now exists merely as one section of a limitless space dimension. Instead of radiators, convectors are located in the side walls or radiating panels on the ceiling. Roofs and balconies extend far into the external space, linking it to the internal one.

59 29. NERVI'S STADIUM AT FLORENCE —AIRCRAFT HANGAR. With some buildings this reaching out into space is a necessary function—for instance with roof structures over railway platforms and over spectator stands in stadia. The cantilevered roof over the seating in the stadium at Florence designed by Nervi and the suspension roof of the aircraft hangar at Lyon, both built in the 1930s, are unsurpassed to this day as examples of cantilever construction.

63 30. STADIUM—STADIUM. The structure of the aircraft hangar at Lyon was reminiscent of suspension bridges, in that they had in common the suspension principle; and so suspension construction principles were considered for utilisation in the enclosure of large spaces, as for example in this project for a stadium in 1927. The main suspension cables are supported by four vertical masts, the piers being formed partly by means of the tiers of stands. A partial realisation of this scheme can be seen in the new stadium at Goetheburg designed by the Swedish architect Janecke. We must remember, too, the suspension roofs of the Schwarzwaldalle and the Wuppertaler.

31. FLIGHT TRAFFIC CONTROL TOWER. It is quite certain that practical requirements are the reason for these 35 wide, cantilevered roof structures; and yet doesn't the almost subconscious desire to defy gravity, to soar, to float on air, underlie all this? Isn't it a new feeling, which the Russian, Malevich, expressed at the beginning of the 1920s in his pictures called 'Flight'? Only pure, functional viewpoints form the basis of Mies van der Rohe's signal box and the project for a traffic control tower.

32. HOUSE BY CORBUSIER—TUBU- 52, 60 LAR STEEL CHAIR. However, the cantilever house by Le Corbusier at the Weißenhofsiedlung, 1927, is to be evaluated as a pure expression of the new feeling. And isn't it remarkable that at that time, simultaneously but completely independently, the suspended tubular steel chair was discovered by three architects in 1926? What really tantalised the technologist was this question: 'What performance is the material capable of?' Gothic vaults, built of stone, are unsurpassable today. But the inherent potentials of new building materials are still a mystery to us.

33. PLYWOOD CHAIR—UMBRELLA 38, 37 HOUSE. The chair illustrated here, made up of 3-mm thick bent plywood and weighing only 2 kg, was made in 1926. Utilising the same principle, and designed at the same time, is this house in reinforced concrete which achieves stability by a spatial folding or moulding, rather as a petal does with its

vaulted form, or as a piece of paper can be transformed by the housewife into a scoop for sugar or flour, simply by folding it.

34. FRANK LLOYD WRIGHT'S TIMBER HOUSE—FALLING WATERS. Indeed the idea of the floating house is already an old one. It was originated by the American architect Frank Lloyd Wright, whose prairie houses of 1914 were remarkable for their cantilevered roofs, balconies, and terraces, their continuous bands of windows, and the totally dominant horizontal emphasis in everything. In these buildings of the 1950s he fully exploited all potentials of the materials for his concepts.

35. FRANK LLOYD WRIGHT'S FALLING WATERS—FLIGHT. Who can help thinking of an aircraft suspended above the waterfall? Were Wright's concepts like those of the Jugendstil poet, Scheerbart? 'The buildings rested like giant butterflies with wings outspread on the edge of cliffs.' A work of the Russian painter Malevitch, done in the 1920s, further illustrates this idea.

36. SUSPENDED RAILWAY—SUSPENDED TOWN. Incidentally, suspended houses already existed before 1900. The only problem was exactly where to suspend them from. For the stations of the Wuppertaler suspended railway, steel frames supporting the roadways were used. In the cartoon illustration by Krause, called 'The town suspended over the Wupper', the high mountains are used as suspension anchors.

37. WILLIAMS—STAM. In a novel written in 1914, *The Grey Cloth*, Paul Scheerbart proposed the erection of 'gallows' from which houses should be hung. Williams of Argentina selects a steel lattice structure similar in form to the system of jacks for lifting a ship, in which the house unit hangs suspended rather like the lift cradle in such gear. In this case it becomes obvious that we are dealing with a round-about construction system, in which the forces

are first of all concentrated at the highest point and only then transferred downwards to the foundations. The simple idea of using vertical, reinforced concrete staircase shafts as the main vertical support from which the various floors could be suspended led to economic propositions; and this picture shows a project by Mart Stamm dated 1956: a house suspended over a street. The main vertical supporting staircase shafts stand on the pavements, and above lies a flat slab from which all the floors are suspended.

38. SUSPENDED HOUSE—APEX. The flat slab mentioned above is the apex of the suspended house and the horizontal member of the gallows, like a cantilever. It is made either of steel or reinforced concrete, and so is an expensive form of construction. In order to justify it, there needs to be a large enough number of storeys to hang from it: therefore suspension building immediately tends towards the form of a skyscraper, as can be seen from the model illustrated here. Incidentally the four tall tower blocks at present under construction in the Civic Centre at Marl are suspended structures and have square plans.

39. TELEVISION TOWER — JOHNSON'S WAX FACTORY. The principle element of the suspension structure is the concrete central core or shaft—which, by the way, is the principle element of any modern tall building, or so-called core structure. It forms the stable vertical structural element, and the television tower near Stuttgart shows just how high such a shaft can be built. The various floors arranged round this shaft don't necessarily have to be suspended forms of construction. In his tower for Johnson's Wax Factory (1950), Frank Lloyd Wright used cantilevered floors, coming out of the central core like branches of a tree. The possibility of cantilevering the floors from the central core in a variety of sizes and shapes, so that the building attains a

123, 61
61
103
109, 106
128
124

82

lively silhouette of horizontally emphasised projecting and recessed elements, was unfortunately not exploited by the architect.

40. SESTRIÈRE—MODEL OF CIRCULAR HOUSE. The most economical form of the cantilever skyscraper—and especially of the suspension structure— is the circular building. The circular building is an old theme much loved by architects, since it takes in the largest area with the smallest external circumference and contains in principle up to twenty per cent more usable area. It was without doubt from the point of view of economy that the newly erected circular skyscrapers in Lyon or Sestrière came about. In the case of the point block suspended structure, the circular building form could be looked upon as the most rational one.

41. INTERBAU MODEL—MODEL OF CIRCULAR HOUSE. At the Interbau Exhibition in 1957 this basic form of suspension building was on view. The staircase is placed within the fireproof central shaft, which therefore forms an easily reached protection area from which one can then calmly descend into the deep cellar, safe from any threatened air raids. Architecturally, the suspension type of construction can be exploited in various ways. If the suspension members are on the exterior they give a vertical emphasis; if they are on the inside, then the elevation would be emphasised horizontally.

42. CAPSTAN—BLOCK PLANNING. As far as Town Planning is concerned, such circular skyscrapers have the advantage of casting the least possible shadow and having the smallest area of their own surfaces in shadow, as well as avoiding the formation of wind tunnels and other wind effects. This example shows the planning of a district having the same population ratio as the one shown in the other illustration which is of block planning dating from 1959.

43. UNTER DEN LINDEN—CARRÉS: BLOCK PLANNING. Block planning is not yet obsolete. The carré, or block planning with internal courtyards or even totally covered-in internal courts, originates basically from the times when buildings were low and traffic meagre. The Roman fort, the soldiers' camp of the Legion, was planned, in principle, like a chequer board. However this was no longer suitable in a period in which traffic at particular points assumed gigantic proportions, while other places remained entirely quiet.

44. CHICAGO—PARIS THOROUGHFARES. There is no doubt that the chequer-board system provides an even traffic distribution, so long as the size and function of the buildings is identical. However, with the accumulation of a larger number of people or goods by particular buildings, some streets were very quickly found to be much too narrow and constantly jammed, whereas others were hardly used; and so the diagonal, wide thoroughfares in Chicago and Paris were laid out to deal with this problem.

45. LINEAR PLANNING—SUSPENSION STRUCTURE CITY.   Linear planning caused a transformation. The town planner tore apart the old unity between house and street: linear planning followed spatial living functions while the street followed the functions of communication. It was only one step further to raise these linear buildings up from the ground, and so achieve a totally open surface area permitting the free development of traffic. **116, 103**

46. HILBESHEIMER — RADBURN. **130, 134** Traffic gradually began to determine our normal day-to-day living. And so it became necessary to build special motorways for it. This started with the ring road round the Potsdamerplatz in 1925 and the construction of the Cloverleaf at New Jersey in 1928. But where did that leave the pedestrian? Hilbesheimer transfers pedestrian traffic

to raised walk-ways, thus isolating him from road traffic, in his Utopian concept of *The City of the Future* (1924). But the first model towns for pedestrians were built in America during the 1930s, for example Radburn and Lindavista. Here we had islands surrounded by traffic arteries. From these ring roads cul-de-sacs lead into the interior of the islands and the houses are placed along these. In the centre of the islands are positioned all the community services, including shops, schools, bus and railway termini, etc. Everything is arranged in such a way that the pedestrian can reach his objective in the shortest possible distance without having any streets to cross.

134, 108 47. ISLAND SCHEME—RIBBON CITY. This scheme, consisting of residential islands, shows a so-called 'island chain' in which residential islands, each of about 500 to 1,000 inhabitants, are strung one alongside the other. The individual islands are surrounded by one-way streets having always a right-hand turn, which necessitates a careful entry system into the two-way highways. In this way, however, the plan functions quite faultlessly without the need for signs, traffic lights, or traffic police. The ribbon city system depends on this principle. In this case the concept is of a city in which it is possible to obtain an unhindered and yet organic expansion potential for each individual zone. Factory zones, manufacturing zones, commercial zones, civic centres, and residential districts are situated on ribbon-like islands which are interconnected by highways. As soon as these ribbons attain a certain length a second highway is made. The ribbons themselves are made up of islands strung next to each other which are surrounded by one-way traffic ring roads. Thus they form so-called 'island chains'. As already remarked, such an arrangement functions without needing warning signals, traffic lights, or traffic police, and is virtually accident free.

84

Unfortunately we did not exploit these possibilities in our destroyed cities, and we are now forced to admit that today we are once again suffering from the same traffic problems which existed before their destruction—but now, unfortunately, with even less chance of solving them.

48. DEPARTMENT STORE—VILLA WALDFRIEDEN. There are two basic building principles, though of quite **95,** different approach: the universally recognised mathematical structure made up of concrete floors and glass walls, and the one-dimensionally limited track of rails, multiple rails, and streets. Now the significance of the linear function was also recognised for other purposes, for example for the organisation of the production line in factories, and for the design of department stores. Everything is arranged so as to be in the closest and most desirable relationship to the person concerned. The problem as to whether or not the ideal apartment should be a machine for living in, in which everything is perfectly arranged and to hand, has been conclusively solved in the affirmative, once and for all, by Krause in his luxury Villa Waldfrieden.

49. HAUS WEHMEIER—WALDFRIE- **135, 1** DEN TEICH. In his design for the Wehmeier house, Krause has also shown how a family with eight children can live and work in such an environment without friction. The same thought and approach has also been extended into the immediate natural external environment; and in this particular case it becomes especially obvious just how much, in an upside-down sort of way, this principle originates in nature, which itself evolves only along an established linear track.

50. BARCELONA PAVILION—BAU- **89** MEISTER'S 'WACHSTUM'. The various parts have become separated from each other and seem to float horizontally in the same plane. The empty space in between gains thereby an especially

high significance. The linear trace of motion has prevailed in painting, exactly as in architecture; and for this reason I end with two works which stand above all functional determination, that is to say, which can be viewed as examples of art for art's sake. The Eiffel Tower was built for its own sake, just as the irrational plan of the Barcelona Pavilion was built for its own sake. But it was done with such complete perfection that one forgets the lack of function and the excessively expensive materials—just as in this picture by Willi Baumeister, which one also does not question in terms of whys or wherefores. It is just the same with technology, which has only been well and truly mastered when one can completely forget about it, or with traffic which does not have to be consciously supervised, or with space when it is perfectly arranged and guarantees the constant maintenance of the objects within it.

Everything illustrated here refers back to the 1920s. Much refers to the Weißenhofsiedlung of 1927. Shall we have the strength and the courage to go a little further along this road?

137   Sketch design by the author as published
in the Bassler and Gormanns catalogue of timber
houses

4. THE ABSOLUTE AND MODULATION

Concerning problems in the creative design of space and surfaces by the artists Oskar Schlemmer and Willi Baumeister during the period between 1937 and 1945. A lecture given at the Werkkunstschule at Kassel on 19th October 1964

Schiller wrote that the arts have as their purpose the creation of illusions or, in the words of Schlemmer, the world of 'as if'. Indeed it seems to be precisely their aim to change appearances, to call into being the opposite of existing reality, or at least to transmute the one into the other.

The empty surface of a sheet of paper is transformed into space by means of only a single dot, Hokusai is supposed to have said 150 years ago. From antiquity right up to the rococo, there was an attempt to achieve an optical recession of walls of narrow rooms, ceilings, and alcoves. The architect tended to do this by using uncontrollable curves in place of measurable corners and edges and also by the use of recesses and openings; the painter, by means of scaled-down compositions or by painting the surfaces black, and so on. Indeed the problem at that time lay in the effort to dissolve the walls into thin air by means of perspective representations and the use of mirrors, that is, to make the physical wall dematerialise and to move it into the inaccessible distance.

But, vice versa, a pane of glass, visually non-existant, can be distinguished by a white mark (the window's invisible boundary marked by a 'No

Smoking' sign); and the dot on the paper surface which we mentioned before is in any case an element which, added to by a second or third, etc., would create a barrier of elements, so that in the end the thin paper surface is visually transformed into a massive body. On a stage, canvas flats visually represent the elemental universe, and thin partition walls in offices and railway carriages can create the impression of a solid enclosure. In these instances the illusion is created by solidifying the insubstantial barrier and moving it into tangible proximity.

As early as 1931, this was the theme of proposals of mine occasioned by Jobst Siedler for the construction (which in fact was never executed) of Hall No. 7, 'Wall and Floor Finishes', for the Berlin Building Exhibition of that year, and I am certain that this would have been a useful contribution. But a few years later in 1937 several artists, who earlier on had already been concerned with the problems of space creation, met in Wuppertal: firstly Willi Baumeister and Oskar Schlemmer, then Krause, and also, later on, Carl Schlemmer and Mucher. There was one exercise which managed to combine in one example the two principles mentioned above, that is the dematerialisation and solidification of walls. In a large staircase enclosure with a front elevation built of glass bricks, the rear and side walls were to be artistically decorated. The long side walls, which were unevenly lit, were made heavy and solid, and the smaller rear wall opposite the glass-brick window was made transparent and light. This was equivalent to the solidification of the lighter separating walls (the side walls) and the dematerialisation of an obtruding wall (the rear wall). And so on the side walls Baumeister painted a mural of differing representations of symbolic content, divided horizontally by means of plastic superimposed layers consisting mainly of white, yellow, and red. In contrast, for the rear wall, Schlemmer had an all-embracing concept of mirror glass, smooth and emphasised vertically, rather like a glass laboratory, in blue and grey. Anyone who has seen the Folkwang slabs at Essen by Schlemmer can perhaps imagine the designs, which have unfortunately been lost. A second exercise, dated 1939, consisted of the painting of two parallel walls, 12 metres long and 5 metres apart, being the side walls of a hall or living room completely open to the garden ; but this did not get beyond the experimental stage. At the time of these sketch designs, Baumeister wrote two theoretical treatises, *The Surface in the Absolute Space* and, *Modulation and Patina*, which he later combined into the single thesis entitled *The Absolute Space and Modulation.*

What do we mean by 'the absolute space' ? An architect will understand by this term the new modern glass skeleton frames without solid walls, which he has not only drawn on a grid but which can be conceived, over and beyond that, as parts of a global space consisting of a total grid of crossing parallel lines and planes. By using the least number of columns and frameworks, he is therefore trying to bring his architecture, consisting as it does of this kind of concept, as close as possible to the

feeling of absolute space. And this is valid, not only for architecture, but also for all commodities which, as is well known, are only the extensions and expansions of our sense apparatus— that is, they can be looked upon as energy-increasing artificial limbs. All space elements strive towards a minimum in material with a maximum in performance.

The painter also takes part in this development. But for his work to have meaning he needs a surface to paint on, and for that reason he needs another type of building technique consisting of walls and partitions, that is, just those things which are becoming more and more scarce as technology continues to develop. Both the architect and the painter really want the same thing. But the absolute space can only be either built or painted : a combination of the two is not possible. With the airy skeleton frame of modern architecture, the painter who wishes merely to represent this sort of thing artificially becomes entirely superfluous. It is extremely unfortunate for the painter who loves to paint murals that in the new skeleton frames of modern architecture there are no solid walls. During the baroque period the painter constantly helped the architect to widen the space of the rooms, to pierce the ceilings ; and Schlemmer looked back full of envy and wonderment to the baroque painters and their work. His work on *The Surface in the Absolute Space* was halted, not only because of his death. He remarked, resignedly, that mural painting, however highly promoted, became extremely questionable in modern architecture. But that is only partly true.

If we admit that modern skeleton frames are only some of the individual parts of an unlimited co-ordinate system, then within this system the walls and floor slabs form dividing planes, inordinately thin, quite without thickness or material properties. Naturally this is not practicable in reality: in the final analysis, floor slabs and walls are fixed barriers and also elements opposing gravity, noise, wind, vision, or light. However, since the dividing planes of a house are only imaginary and therefore infinitely thin, so the architect, when solidifying them for various purposes, also seeks to make them as thin as possible, if only in order to avoid reducing room sizes unnecessarily. The thinnest plane we are familiar with, however, is the layer of pigment applied by the painter, and we have already mentioned earlier on that this thin layer can give an impression of the heaviest material. Let us have another, closer look. How is a surface revealed? I think it is by means of its colour and structure. By colour we differentiate between warm and cold and accordingly judge this wall, or that analogous object, to be nearer or farther away. In the case of structures, there are in existence regular ones (textures, plough furrows, honeycombs), or irregular ones (marble, tree bark, sand dunes)—during the 1920s the favourite examples were sponge cakes and bread crusts, and later on for both kinds Baumeister showed lantern slides of moving water surfaces made by Lauterwasser, the photographer. Here, as Baumeister so rightly remarked, we are dealing with a cumulative effect. This surface phenomenon is brought about by the painter in various ways: by means of modelling, or by means of modulation. Modelling (or moulding) imitates spatial realities by means of contours and shadow projection, and relies on our knowledge of the spatial universe. Modulation, on the other hand, permits materials to achieve immediate expression: only the influences on materials are controlled. With colour, consistency, method of application, regulated forms of expression are produced, formations which do not conceal their means of creation and so transform the abstract plane into

manifestations of the solid universe familiar to our senses. Thus we experience hard and soft, elation and depression, wet and dry, near and far, rough and smooth, etc. With their manufactured experimental tablets (several hundred in number), Baumeister, Schlemmer and Krause did not pursue any definite, practical purpose, but only wanted to establish a catalogue of all the modulative possibilities. However their effect, when studied, is not merely to make one quite involuntarily say that they look 'as if . . .', and wonder, how would this one look in this or that space—on the contrary, these tablets are capable of transmitting their own individual aesthetic experience, since they are the individual autographs of highly gifted artists.

However, Baumeister contends that nothing can be thought of which does not exist in nature; and for once we can believe this without reservations, since what we know forms only a minute part of reality. A film of oil crystals was shown during the opening of the Bauhaus at Dessau in 1926. Microphotographs of the crystalline structure of metals are just as strange and unfamiliar as pictures of distant galaxies. Nevertheless the painter constantly discovers things which we have overlooked, such as the appearance of patina, of decay, of dissolution, a process during which not only do surprising modulations occur, but also more permanent things are discovered which are often more valid than the transient ones. But the patina is in any case only a manifestation of the material world which we include under the comprehensive concept of 'nature', and the process of creation belongs to this, too. 'Nature' is a picture of constant metamorphosis, the basis of all nature; so in this sense the artist does nothing which differs from what nature does herself in that, exactly as she does, he creates modulations and either adds them to, or fits them in with, hers. In this way modulation and patina are (quoting Baumeister) more than just related in their intrinsic qualities: they are born of one and the same mother and are therefore twins. As an analogy to this, the artist finds his new means of self-expression. Cézanne gave us a command: Modulate—don't model. And by this he pointed to regularity of plane and colour application. One was to divide the painting surface into portions, take it to pieces, make a mosaic of it, and make as many bigger or smaller areas as one wished to fit together in one's field of vision and which suited the painting tool. In this way one explored what was actually true—for instance, that lighter and red planes appear to be nearer, and darker and blue planes tend to recede. So from this mosaic was produced a type of relief painting formed by the varied treatment of adjacent planes. A relief painting is a physical wall.

This transformation of the surface by the use of structure and colour became the most important means of creation in modern painting. And, inevitably, painters were not satisfied with this, but sought to explode the solid structure of this surface even further. Baumeister says, 'The bomb must explode' or 'The cake must be crumbled, what sticks together must be disintegrated, the plane must be perforated, torn apart, and the figures separated from each other'. However, to be able to do this at all, one must understand the elements, and learn the need to confine oneself to these alone: the basic foundation, the material to be added to or applied to it, the equipment with which this is done, the holding of the equipment, the practised pressure, the quicker or slower motion of the hand, and the effort expended. A hair brush, charged with quickly evaporating water-colour, when applied to an extremely sensitive paper surface, needs to be moved across the paper quickly and lightly. For this reason such a technique is well suited to catching fleeting impressions quickly. A rougher foundation, a more viscous painting material, a bristle brush, force one into a slower tempo and bring about a more precise control. The pen flies over the smooth paper; the much harder needle scratches into the metal; still more obstinate is the carving of the knife into the wood block. Every drawing, etching, woodcut, must allow one to recognise the process of its creation, and, even further, it is from this that the expression must spring if the statement is to have any validity. Of course this imposes a certain limitation, but one can't do everything at once. In any case the eye, from all its impressions, only remembers certain properties—sometimes it may be colour, sometimes form. One can easily see from the creative efforts of a child how dependent our communication is on the technical means which bring it about. Using colours, one will only represent the colours of the impression one has received, as for instance a green area of paint representing a tree, or a red one representing brickwork. With a pencil, on the other hand, one would represent only shapes and lines. We may quite possibly have discovered form and colour only through painting or drawing exercises, or have learned to see it only by the circuitous route of becoming a painter; and perhaps if we didn't have any colour materials for use in representation, but only scoring tools, we might never really see the world in terms of colour.

The formation of surfaces is raised to a material reality through the non-veiled, non-figurative, non-allusive revelation of technical means, as of the elements. And this is precisely the opposite of what was done in previous centuries, when architects built caves, and painters extended them with illusionary tricks, realistically or surrealistically, so that it was no great distance from the baroque ceiling with its painted heaven to the peep-show or Madame Tussaud's.

The absolute and modulation are not a conceptual dichotomy such as hot and cold, white and black, near and far. The idea of absolute or mathematical space is the opposite of that of relative or substance-filled space by which we understand a reality made up of denser and more tenuous substance in such a way that, in the case of two substances or materials situated next to each other, we describe as 'space' the one which loses its characteristic shape or form when the two are moved together, whilst the other, which keeps its shape, is called 'the body'. Thus water becomes space for a body such as a hand. Air is a space for a body such as a drop of water. The relative space is determined through motions and relationships; it always depends on such a 'body' and its expansion is generated by means of this body. Absolute space, however, is the same everywhere. It remains static.

Modulation, as we have already seen in quotations from Cézanne's writings, has as its opposite modelling or moulding. And to put it more precisely, in Schlemmer's words: Modulation and patina are the outward manifestations of materials, of nature. Modelling imitates the various forms without thereby possessing any individual, characteristic substance which is not part of the copy. Its substantial character is the absolute plane, which was Schlemmer's aim in his paintings at various periods. However, Baumeister found that, just as in architecture the old concept of the cave space had been swept aside by the new concept of absolute space, so modelling would have to give way to modulation. The modern concept would then become determined by the absolute and modulation. Both contain aspects of reality. Modulation contains the fullness of natural phenomena as well as all that is individual. The absolute, in contrast, contains simply space and that which has become standardised, and, in addition, the quality of 'standard', that is, the perfection or completeness of a building or tool which excludes any further alterations, as for instance in the case of the much-quoted bicycle.

Just such an ultimate form was sought by Schlemmer for his pictures— a form in which the absolute, that is the surface which has become dematerialised, is indicated by shapes which float within it, and finally merely as large or small (that is, nearer or farther) lights. His pictures were supposed to be 'from out of time and space', meaning that they were to look as though no human hand had taken any part in their creation, or that the 'unfortunate human hand' was as insignificantly recognisable in them, as in some perfect industrial tool. Perhaps he really meant the 'clumsy' human hand in this context, since he is obviously thinking of the concept which we understand by 'perfect', namely an almost immaterial, unblemished state.

An unusual sequence of ideas followed. Man-made things, both functional such as buildings and tools, and artistic, should fit in with nature in such a way that they would actually seem a part of nature. There are instances, says Schlemmer, where nature has reached a point of rest and gives us a glimpse of absolute space. The perfect star-covered night sky, snow-covered ground, water reflections, crystals—all are parts of the absolute which have become visible. In a similar way the pyramids and the cupolas of the Pantheon and Hagia Sophia are also parts of the absolute, serving as a contrast to natural growth and springing from the same soil, as also do bridges, roads, ships, cars and aircraft.

From his different point of view, Baumeister reached a similar conclusion. Modulation, as he says, is supposed to be as natural as a signature, so that it fits into nature without any leftovers, in exactly the same way as a beautiful natural rock would fit in, or a piece of driftwood, or a naturally weathered brick wall, or an old ruin. And this is only possible if modulation permits recognition of the creative process in terms of temporal components, as these examples do. Nature's phenomena are her statements; and, with all his technical aids, man's statements do not differ from hers. A statement is the natural, unembroidered expression of feeling and judgment. According to Baumeister, such a statement is purer, the more simple and unequivocable the technology by which it is expressed. And (not least for this reason) man's discovery of expression is most moving in prehistoric remains and in the artefacts of primitive races. On the one hand we find it in flint tools or dolmens, on the other in South Sea tapas or Chinese calligraphy. In this way statements of the human spirit and heart become an orderly whole and fit in harmoniously with existing nature.

Schlemmer and Baumeister started with different ideas, but worked towards the same goal. If we want to express it in one short statement, then perhaps we might put it like this: Out of the intellectual ideal of the absolute and the material adventure of modulation, two different streams of art sprang up to enrich our concept of nature. However, I do agree with Baumeister in this—it is easier to do than to say, and easier to say than to understand.

some roots of modern architecture